THROUGH THEIR EYES

Through Their Eyes

A Community History of Eagle, Circle, and Central

Michael Koskey, Laurel Tyrrell, and Varpu Lotvonen

UNIVERSITY OF ALASKA PRESS

Published by
University of Alaska Press
P.O. Box 756240
Fairbanks, AK 99775-6240

Cover design by Kristina Kachele
Interior design by Rachel Fudge

Cover image by Patrick Endres, AlaskaStock.com (#103AR CM0004D001)

Library of Congress Cataloging-in-Publication Data
Names: Koskey, Michael Stephen, author. | Tyrrell, Laurel Beach, author. |
    Lotvonen, Varpu, author.
Title: Through their eyes : a community history of Eagle, Circle, and Central /
    Michael Koskey, Laurel Tyrrell, and Varpu Lotvonen.
Description: Fairbanks, AK : University of Alaska Press, [2018] | Includes bib-
    liographical references and index. |
Identifiers: LCCN 2017059949 (print) | LCCN 2018030712 (ebook) | ISBN
    9781602233584 (e-book) | ISBN 9781602233577 (pbk. : alk. paper)
Subjects: LCSH: Alaska—Social life and customs. | Eagle (Alaska)—History. |
    Circle (Alaska)—History. | Yukon-Koyukuk Census Area (Alaska)—History.
Classification: LCC F904.6 (ebook) | LCC F904.6 .K67 2018 (print) | DDC
    979.8—dc23
LC record available at https://lccn.loc.gov/2017059949

Contents

List of Illustrations

Acknowledgments

MANY GENEROUS PEOPLE were involved in various ways and degrees with this project, and to all the following (and those who may be overlooked here), we thank you for your help, expertise, and interest.

Special thanks to Isaac Juneby, former chief and Elder of Eagle Village, whose assistance was needed and valued throughout the project. Isaac was lost in an automobile accident during the last phases of this project (summer 2012), and this work is dedicated to him, his efforts to educate and inform others about his Hän people, his work to revitalize and teach the Hän language, and his tireless effort to improve the lives of the people of his community. Isaac was an inspiration and a leader for Hän and non-Hän people alike, and he always generously provided his time and knowledge.

Residents past and present of Eagle City, Eagle Village, Central, and Circle also provided support. From Eagle, John Borg, Mike McDougall, Terry McMullin, Ruth Ridley, Sonja Sager, and Donald Woodruff provided important knowledge based on their considerable experience and expertise; special thanks to Eagle resident Pat Sanders of Yukon–Charley Rivers National Preserve for her extensive knowledge, rigorous reviews, and editing. From Central, Silvia Boullion, Alfred Cook, William and

Collette Glanz, Robert Miller, Theresa Ordway, Richard Tyrrell, Frank and Mary Warren, and Lori Wilde all generously provided their knowledge, expertise, and/or photographs on the topics covered in this work. Special thanks to Jane Williams of Central, who provided considerable information and editing for this publication. From Circle, Albert Ames, Molly Ames, Jeannie Boyle, and Charles John provided important information about life in the Yukon–Charley region. Finally, at the University of Alaska Fairbanks, the College of Rural and Community Development and the Department of Alaska Native Studies and Rural Development provided considerable administrative support, as did the Center for Cross-Cultural Studies.

This project was initially made possible by funding from the National Park Service through the efforts and oversight of David Krupa. Critical to the success of this effort were project partners and coauthors Laurel Tyrrell of Central and Varpu Lotvonen, research assistant and graduate student at the University of Alaska Fairbanks.

Thanks to you all!

ONE

Shared Traditions

The People, the Land, the River

S OME TIME AGO, in the early years of the twenty-first century, an
Alaska Native man—a local leader—was asked to try to explain his
understanding of what traditional knowledge meant to him. In front of a
room filled with government bureaucrats, and with few of his own Hän
Hwëch'in people present, this guest began by slowly walking to the front
of the room, visibly nervous in spite of countless years of survival in the
Alaska woods, in spite of years of recognized leadership and formal educational achievements, and in spite of the widespread admiration of him
shown by friends and strangers alike. Bearing himself with dignity and
pride but cloaked in humility and deference to those around him—equals
in all ways to him, in his mind—Isaac Juneby, of the community of Eagle,
stood for a moment thinking of the best way to try to explain his notion
of knowledge to the room of college-educated professionals, from communities across the United States and Canada, who had come together
in this meeting. Knowing nothing of the lives of most people in the audi-
ence, Isaac began his explanation:

> You see, somebody asked me, "What is traditional knowledge?" That's
> the first thing they would ask me and I couldn't go to a dictionary
> because there's no meaning there. So I said, "It is that what is instilled

within my heart from learning; somebody teaching me," and I know that in the Western philosophy of education, a lot of the things we learn is by reading. Well, this one—traditional knowledge—is a passed-on deal. It's word of mouth. And it's also values; what values I know about traditional knowledge. And I'm a collective owner of that type [of knowledge]. It's not like, say, I can write about it and become famous because this is what it is right here—life, survival. It's a value system within the way that I think, and I project it. By that I mean that it's also used in experience and observation…(Upper Tanana Cultural Resource Summit, March 22–23, 2005)

In this same way, Isaac explained to those involved in compiling and writing this ethnohistorical account that the way things are "recorded in books and on paper" isn't the "true truth," as he stated it, but "one of many truths that people believe with equal sureness." When people remember events of their lives, the realization revealed is that individuals carry many worldviews, and that these worldviews help to shape their beliefs and their experiences of the world. Isaac recognized that knowledge is derived from where worldviews overlap, and where they do not, and so each person possesses knowledge that others do not. Each person has something to teach, and each person has more to learn; traditional knowledge "recognizes" this, and so through humility can one best learn about something. Fully aware of this condition, Isaac sought to help write a history of the people of the central-eastern Interior of Alaska from their own perspectives. To facilitate this effort, many people were interviewed in the villages of Central, Circle, and Eagle—the three principle communities of the central-eastern Interior. This book is the culmination of Isaac's efforts, in cooperation with the authors of this text.

Subsistence Livelihoods and Mixed Economies

This is a story of the people of a region—the central-eastern Interior of Alaska—and through the people we can draw general conclusions about their history, their lives, and their place in the contemporary world. Through the lives of the characters who are historical and local people, an account of the region is revealed. As a series of shared experiences, this work is historical and traditional knowledge—the way the people remember the happenings of their lives, and of those with whom their lives have been shared. Such a reckoning as this is an ethnohistory—a history of a *people* rather than of a political entity, such as a country or government. This ethnohistory represents and depicts the past from the point of view and perspective of those who lived it, through their own recollections and recordings or through the records, recordings, and remembrances of those who were their peers or later chroniclers.

We will meet many people from Alaska's central-eastern Interior from the three communities of Eagle, Circle, and Central, and each adds to their community's and the region's history. Many are mentioned in passing, in historical reference, or through the accounts of others, but each community focus will feature one or more residents through whom these stories are largely, though not exclusively, recounted. In Eagle, we focus on Isaac Juneby, introduced above, who was a longtime leader and Elder of the Hän people who dwell in Eagle alongside a settler population. Isaac, like the others to be introduced, was adept at living in both worlds—that of Alaska Natives and that of settlers originally from outside Alaska. In Circle, we focus on Albert Carroll, a leader and Elder of the Gwichyaa Gwich'in people, who knew well the particulars of the channels, sloughs, and dangers of the Yukon River. One of the authors of this text, Laurel Tyrrell, a longtime resident of Central, a local historian and teacher, trapper, and hunter, is also featured alongside the historical accounts of the Larsen and Olson families, who were some of the first settlers in the region. Through their eyes, and those of the many community members interviewed for this project, is this ethnohistory created.

Much of the information gained in an ethnohistorical work is derived from oral traditions—especially oral history. These oral historical accounts are then put in their historical place both in their proper time period (chronologically) and also according to other relations with other events and people. Since this work is most fundamentally an account of the lifeways of the indigenous and settler populations of the region, it is told through their accounts, supplemented by recorded accounts from historical, government, church, and other documents. The recollections and oral histories through which an ethnohistorical account is created serve to tie together historical documentary evidence and reckoning with local events and perspectives, thereby personalizing historical developments and people's experiences of them.

Formally, ethnohistory is a branch of cultural studies (usually within anthropological contexts) that focuses on the history of peoples and cultures rather than on historical documents that largely reflect the perspectives of the society's privileged individuals, families, or institutions—often those who write history and control the narrative through the authoring function. This is not to say that formal historical documents written by authors looking in from the outside are dismissed, or that the privileged in society are not relevant to a history of a people, but that these are supplemented by oral accounts of events as remembered by community-respected and recognized knowledge bearers from within all portions of a society's population. In this way an ethnohistory is the history of a people rather than being limited to a history of their polities, their elites, their dominant institutions, and their achievements and conflagrations. An ethnohistory, then, is an account of a people's history from multiple—ideally all—portions of their society.

Ethnohistorians recognize the value of maps, music, paintings, photography, folklore, oral tradition, ecology, site exploration, archaeological materials, museum collections, enduring customs, language, and place names (Axtell 1979, 3–4). By taking the time to learn knowledge of the defined group, including through linguistic insights and an understanding of cultural phenomena, this makes for a more in-depth analysis than if research is based only on written documents (Lurie 1961, 83). Ethnohistorical research attempts to understand a culture on its own terms and according to its own cultural values, expressions, and worldviews. Axtell described ethnohistory as "the use of historical and ethnological methods to gain knowledge of the nature and causes of change in a culture defined by ethnological concepts and categories" (Axtell 1979, 2). Ethnohistory must fundamentally take into account the people's own understanding of how events are constituted, including their ways of culturally constructing the past. Simmons formulated his understanding of ethnohistory as "a form of cultural biography that draws upon as many kinds of testimony as possible over as long a time period as the sources allow," and it is based on a holistic, diachronic approach that is "joined to the memories and voices of living people" (Simmons 1988, 10).

Pivotal to this document as an ethnohistory and apparent throughout this text is the notion, as portrayed by Isaac's insight, that the sharing of knowledge is a reflection of the sharing of culture in general. This is evident throughout the historical narrative and discussion, and this sharing—directly tied to the immigration of settlers into the region—led early to the emergence of conditions of interdependence between indigenous peoples and settlers. As settlers arrived, their economic activities, essentially resource extraction, differed greatly from those of the local indigenous peoples, who relied greatly on subsistence. Soon after arrival, however, many non-Natives learned how to survive in the unfamiliar country by learning traditional knowledge from Alaska Natives—critically important for success in what seemed to settlers to be the edge of the world. Likewise, soon after the settlers' arrival, the local indigenous people began participating in the economic activities of the settlers, including woodcutting for fuel for riverboats, trapping for fur sales to outside buyers, and providing supplies and transport for gold prospectors and others. Through the cross-cultural experiences now long common to the region, a condition has arisen of interdependency—shared experiences characterized by persistence and change. The familiarity with the lands and waters of the region is a common trait among its residents, though how they depend on the land differs between cultures.

Such cross-cultural contact often gradually leads to a common set of values—at least in part—and this can help to develop and maintain respect in cross-cultural interactions. The learning, and sometimes adoption, of others' customs helps to break down social and intellectual barriers that lead to misunderstandings, prejudices, and racism. For example, Isaac Juneby of Eagle pursued a formal Western education to better enable him to work with and understand non-Native government and bureaucracy. Albert Carroll developed into a widely respected riverboat pilot. Laurel Tyrrell was a schoolteacher and earned a master's degree, though she is also a successful subsistence provider. Isaac and Albert, too, continued their subsistence activities throughout their lives. Each one crossed cultures to learn from others, resulting in improved self-sufficiency through expansion of skills while recognizing and maintaining social links through sharing and interdependent support. This pattern can be seen throughout this eastern region of rural Alaska and is representative of processes of social cooperation throughout the North in Alaska and Canada.

This ethnohistory focuses on the central-eastern Interior of Alaska because the rapid changes seen in the region, especially from mining but also from other activities, accentuates the potential for culture clash. The central-eastern Interior is a unique region of northwestern North America that experienced rapid changes due to the presence of nearby mining districts, including the famed Klondike to the east. A cold, dry, rugged region of high plateaus, hills, and boreal forest interspersed with lakes and marshes, the central-eastern Interior is sparsely populated by any standard but provides well for those who are familiar with its lands and waters. Interest in similar resources brings different peoples together, creating economic interdependencies that prove beneficial to all involved.

Crossing the region from southeast to northwest are the Yukon River and its important tributaries—especially Birch Creek and the Fortymile River—which connect the communities of the area. Eagle and Circle lie directly on the Yukon River while Central lies near Birch Creek (more a river than a creek), a tributary of the Yukon. The Yukon figures prominently in the cultures of the central-eastern Interior and also ties the communities together conceptually. Through the focus on the three communities of the area—Eagle, Central, and Circle—the interdependency that enables success in this otherwise-harsh land is a central ethic of local people, particularly through the custom of sharing, and this is especially emphasized culturally among Alaska Natives.

The central-eastern Interior has long been the home of indigenous Athabascan peoples—Alaska Natives—including the Hän Hwёch'in and Gwichyaa Gwich'in (both Athabascan, or more properly Dené or Dena, peoples). For the last 120 years or so, the region has also been the home of settlers from outside Alaska. While the vast majority of these settlers arrived from the United States, many also came from Canada or Europe (and, in modern times, increasingly from the Pacific Rim). In spite of very

different origins, worldviews, and spiritual traditions, indigenous and settler groups share a surprising number of similarities, especially in the lifeways practiced in the region. These include subsistence hunting, fishing,
and trapping; large-scale woodcutting for the sternwheelers (riverboats);
and, of course, gold mining.

Alaska Natives also participated in mining, though it was not common for them to have direct ownership of claims. In the beginning,
subject to the sometimes-capricious judgment of the individual miners'
associations that constituted early law enforcement, some associations
did not permit Alaska Natives to own claims, while others voted to allow
such ownership, and still others switched positions over time. For example, the two miners who first discovered gold on Birch Creek in 1893
were of mixed descent (Native and non-Native). Sergei Cherosky and
Pitka Pavaloff's original discovery spot was "rediscovered"[1] by three non-
Natives. Cherosky and Pavaloff later recorded other claims on Deadwood
Creek but apparently lost the claim at the original discovery site due to
their Russian and Alaska Native heritage. It is presumed that the mining associations in the Deadwood Creek area must have voted to "allow"
them to own their claims there.

As pursuits such as mining led local indigenous peoples to participate
in new activities, indigenous peoples also influenced local settlers—particularly in areas of survival. Oftentime, it was the descendants of mixed
marriages who formed the cultural bridge between two distinct lifeways
and cultures. These individuals, while little noticed in official records, are
sometimes well remembered in local accounts and stories. These include
Hän leader Isaac Juneby from Eagle and his wife, Sandra, from Chicago,
and Albert Carroll's father, James A. Carroll, from Minnesota and his
Gwich'in wife, Fannie, from Fort Yukon. Before these, pioneer traders
Mayo, McQuesten, and Harper also married Alaska Native women.

Essential to this work is a collection of local stories combined with
documented events and lifeways that together provide a picture of the
region's history from a community perspective. Through these stories,

---

1   According to the Sam Dunham report of 1893, the three non-Natives were Gus
Williams, John McLeod, and Henry Lewis.

the interdependency of local peoples, whatever their cultural origins, is apparent. Informal knowledge of place, process, belief, and craft was shared. This interdependence and resulting cultural mixing is a process that continues to the present. Understanding how and why this occurs is relevant to the American experience as a whole—an experience that has characterized the entire history of the United States and Canada, and that presently includes Alaska. One of the most obvious reflections of this process is the personal oral histories of individuals who are participants in this process, including indigenous peoples and settlers. Here is an account of these local people, informed by recognized knowledge bearers from among the people themselves. And as the events of history change the nature of a person's and a group's identity, the knowledge they bear—traditional, local, and/or indigenous—changes as well. Traditions should be understood for what they are: customs that are practiced by multiple people across generations, not as anachronisms of the past. Likewise, traditional knowledge is flexible, ever changing, and not necessarily limited to a particular culture or ethnic group, even though a culture or community is often the source of its origin. A local perspective, too, is evident in the stories that inform this ethnohistorical work and that are described throughout this account. Essentially, this is a people's perspective of their own history. An ethnohistorical approach is also important in demonstrating how issues of change are not abstract. Awareness and, ideally, understanding of local contexts and perspectives are applied constantly through the daily life of individuals and groups.

Throughout the course of this work, many local residents were interviewed and consulted, and these personal accounts serve to qualify official documentation. Most interview respondents were elderly, many were middle-aged, and some were young; these residents' accounts provide detail to the stories that together comprise the histories of Central, Circle, and Eagle, Alaska. Here we have an integrated account of these three central-eastern Interior communities and the historical ties that brought them together. The most important two factors that bind these communities are the Yukon River and its tributaries, which are their transportation highway, and the quest for gold that unleashed the influx of settlers.

More recently, the Steese Highway (and its predecessor trails) became an important link binding together the communities of Circle and Central and connecting them with Fairbanks, a lifeline for goods and services not accessible within the communities. A final element joins the three communities: each is situated near the borders of the Yukon–Charley Rivers National Preserve, created in 1980. The preserve comes with regulations and opportunities for seasonal employment, and attracts visitors from around the world. Many changes accompanied the establishment of Yukon–Charley Rivers National Preserve, affecting the right of access and subsistence activities within the preserve.

These changes are in addition to those brought to the region with the arrival of explorers, trappers, miners, and others over the past century and a half, affecting everything from clothing and diet to beliefs and technologies. As a result, indigenous Hän Hwëch'in and Gwichyaa Gwich'in have seen their cultures undergo rapid and sometimes debilitating change with the influx of new lifeways, new religion, new languages, and new authorities, most of which were imposed on the region and its people without local consent. Nevertheless, in many cases both Alaska Natives and non-Natives have benefited from economic development. Considered by most outsiders to be isolated and underpopulated, the central-eastern Interior continues to be a place where the effects of the global economy and global awareness press upon the freedoms otherwise allowed by isolation. Together, the peoples of the region and the National Park Service are defining a new condition of cooperation and competition in Alaska's rugged Interior.

The maintenance of a people's self-definition and identity is difficult under the conditions of rapid social change experienced due to colonization. In its modern sense, colonization includes the imperial activities over the past five hundred years wherein some countries economically exploited others through conquest and/or the plantation of settlements, resulting in the domination of the colonizer over the colonized, thereby threatening notions of identity. One way to maintain identity is to provide a public space for people to tell their story from their own perspective, and to allow for self-determination within such a space (in addition to their own traditional spaces). In this book we have worked to blend existing accounts and research—both oral and written—with new accounts from recently arrived residents and from lifelong and long-term residents. In doing this blending, our guiding principle was to respect the interests and perspectives of the people at the center of this study.

With a local focus in mind, this ethnohistory will be told in part through the eyes of a few featured residents who are recognized by their communities as both knowledge bearers and leaders. From this personal perspective, the stories that make up the histories of the region are brought together under specific themes: gold mining, wood-cutting, hunting, fishing, trapping, and transportation and trade activities. Of course, the means of livelihood change from time to time as technologies and market demands have changed, and so these topics are followed through time from their rise to their demise, or to their continuation in the present. As is evident from the activities mentioned above, and with the changing economies that rise and fall in the region according to outside needs or interests, the local economy has long been characterized by diversity, resiliency, and complexity, involving a mix of subsistence activities, resource exploration and extraction, and wage labor, consistently augmented by sharing and exchange of goods. Most locals participate in all these activities as needs demand or opportunity allows.

One of the most important goals of this book is to show the interdependence that has arisen from culture contact and culture change. Interdependence is the blending of traditions and worldviews as well as the personal and cultural ties to the land that are part of most rural cultures. The story of interdependence between Alaska Natives and settlers is built through relationships, though the nature of these relationships can vary greatly. Indeed, a connection to community, land, water, and the creatures therein forms part of the worldviews of rural Alaskans, whether indigenous or settler, and many participate in subsistence activities that help to foster a sort of interconnected self-sufficiency. Such cultural and social independence alongside interdependence can be readily found in the three communities of focus in this ethnohistory: Eagle, Central, and Circle.

Subsistence Livelihoods and Mixed Economies

Critical to this ethnohistorical account is the need to understand the role of subsistence lifeways and people's involvement in the local, regional, national, and global cash-based economies. Today, a subsistence hunter uses clothing and tools usually made elsewhere in the world and acquired through monetary exchange. The reality of Alaska's rural economies is that they are mixed, with subsistence activities and wage labor existing side-by-side. The historical accounts that make up this work reveal that this is not a recent trend but a long-term development that has its origins in the Russian, British and French Canadian, and American merchant-adventurers who came to the area to trade. These visitors and settlers also traded for sustenance and amenities that were essential to the support of trapping and mining, and for this subsistence hunters were also important.

The subsistence lifeway is heavily based on traditional and/or local knowledge, and this knowledge is firmly anchored in the individual's—and therefore the community's—relationship with the land and its nonhuman persons. The term *nonhuman persons* indicates a worldview that conceives of all existence having "spirit" or "awareness" in the sense of each being a unique and meaningful entity—essentially an animistic concept that presumes all things possess spirit, and that spirit is often seen as being ultimately unitary (panentheistic) with all others. Traditional knowledge is, of course, not the things produced by it but the sum of the understanding of the natural, social, and spiritual environments in which a group of people dwell. Local knowledge is tradition, no matter what its cultural origin, and as with traditional knowledge, it is not static but instead a gradual and dynamic reaction to the place of a human group's residence over time and generations. Subsistence activities must adapt to changes in the land itself caused by natural cycles such as flood or fire, including climate change that may be the cause of irregular fire and floods. Many local hunters, trappers, fishers, and others are consistently exposed to and aware of these changes in Alaska, and a great many report changing climatic trends, including warmer winters and less snowfall overall. Climate change affects not only the weather and land but also those who live on the land, including animals and the humans who rely on them for subsistence (Hinzman et al. 2005,

280–283). Not only can migration patterns change, but so species composition can change over the long term. Such changes can have profound effects on human cultures, and as the environment and its inhabitants are altered, so too are lifeways potentially changed. While most cultures are capable of adapting to such changes, rapid culture change—whether as a result of climate change or another causal factor—often leads to sociocultural disruption in the short term and significant cultural changes in the long term. This is succinctly expressed in a recent climate change study by Hinzman et al. (2005):

> Changes in traditional patterns of harvest of fish and wildlife by indigenous peoples may be necessary as distribution of species change with changes in habitat characteristics. For example, availability of moose may increase and caribou decrease in the northern boreal forest as a consequence of increased fire and insect epizootics… Adaptability will be a key element in living in a changing Arctic. An integrated assessment of Arctic community sustainability involving scientists and Native communities modeled possible forces for change, including a warming climate, to ascertain their implications to Old Crow, Yukon Territory, a small Gwich'in community with no road access that is highly dependent on Porcupine caribou… A warming climate is likely to have a negative population effect on caribou availability by affecting access to hunting grounds… (284)

Local residents have commented upon changes such as new small trees beginning to grow in places that did not have any trees when they were young, which changes the behavior of animals such as caribou. When there was no growth, caribou ran through these places, but now they stop to graze, making harvesting them easier. Lakes that flood and do not drain and others that were lakes and have since dried up now cover the landscape. New channels that bypass the sloughs moose live on can disrupt access and movement patterns. Fires drastically change the land formations and vegetation in areas that burn. Moose will feed elsewhere until the new growth of willows and birch, after ten or eleven years, attract them back to feed in the burned areas. Beaver move as well to new locations outside the fire areas to find new feed until the growth returns. All these changes require the subsistence practitioner to change hunting and trapping efforts to successfully adapt to the change.

Such adaptations favor sustainability and resilience in most cases and tend to avoid behaviors that foster overexploitation or socioeconomic privilege. In this holistic and interdependent way, the approach to social and ecological concerns is qualified by cultural and spiritual concerns, and each aspect serves to inform the others. As a family or group of families travel together over and over again across the land, they remember, pass on, talk about, teach, and create stories of experiences in specific locations: "This is where Grandma fell through the ice on her sno-go [snowmobile]; good thing it is not very deep but the ice is thin in this spot"; "When the wind blows from the southwest, it will cause a drift to form here that will block the highway"; "Could be four or five feet deep: moose usually follow this drainage in the fall as they migrate from the hills to the flats"; "It is a good place to hunt."

A culture's relationship to the land serves, in part, to define its members' behavior toward the land, leading to the rise of a social value of either conservation or exploitation. In reality, this social value usually falls somewhere in between. The indigenous peoples of the central-eastern Interior perceive their relation to the land to be deeply rooted in their experiences and those of their ancestors, and the local environmental value is an ethic of respect and reverence. This provides space for the development of cultural values and behaviors that reflect this ethic—especially sharing in the form of reciprocity (giving and receiving in balance). One of the most important demonstrations of respect and reverence, reciprocity displays the individual's concern for the well-being of another and, practically, helps to ensure one's own well-being reciprocally. Reciprocity is vitally important for developing social relationships, and these relationships can be critical to survival, particularly during disasters. Sharing is not performed without the expectation of return—reciprocation is expected at some imprecise future time and without much concern for monetary value. In fact, there is an element of pride involved in that one does not receive without giving in return. In a contemporary context, Isaac Juneby demonstrated this "patient reciprocity" in Fairbanks when the young man he had generously helped with food and cash was observed offering to chop and haul firewood in return, later offering again to wash dishes through a potlatch. And while reciprocity can be performed with cash—essentially a resource—the meaning of the reciprocation continues to be rooted in the exchange itself.

Those who have settled the lands in recent times have also widely come to accept and add their own customs to an ethic of sharing, even if the relationship with the land differs spiritually. The effects are similar, and it is recognized that if the land and waters or their inhabitants are treated disrespectfully—through overexploitation or careless pollution—negative consequences should be expected. As one longtime resident of the Circle-Central region said, "Can't think of anybody who'd go out and deliberately destroy the land. Who would? ... If you live out in the woods you take care of it. You don't throw your dirty things in the river" (H95-09-01 and 02). While unfortunately this attitude is not universal, it does characterize the perspective of most who depend directly on the land and waters for sustenance and survival.

Economic Conditions

Economic capacities and opportunities have always determined the scale of human presence in the region, including the indigenous subsistence economies in which abundance or lack of resources determined the size and location of human populations. Every day, individuals bring to bear their cultural, educational, and experiential skills to make a living. The mixed subsistence–cash economy reflects the recognition and understanding of the socioeconomic conditions found in the region. In a web of interdependence, subsistence activities now serve to inform and augment cash-based economic decisions, and cash-based economic opportunities serve to increase access to and enhance subsistence-based economic interests. This is not, or need not be, a struggle between two worldviews or economic traditions. Instead, it is simply the way of the present, as real and likely as enduring as the economic lifeways that preceded this mixed economy. Such a condition of economic interdependence and integration, of course, means that local economic processes may be more familiar to outsiders than in the past, but it also indicates that the current subsistence-oriented cash economy at the local level is more complicated than is often understood.

A complete understanding of the nuances and meanings of the subsistence lifeway requires active participation in it. It is one thing to learn about hunting, fishing, trapping, survival, and other skills, but to transform such information into knowledge, one must practice the skill and participate in the activity. Such involvement, when combined with some knowledge of a people's worldview, including notions of cosmology and ontology, can enable a deeper understanding of a people's customs and behaviors, perspectives and awareness(es). In the context of the central-eastern Interior of Alaska, this is largely accomplished through involvement in subsistence activities. Naturally, the opposite is true, where knowledge can be gained about mining, commerce, transportation, and government through involvement in these.

The practice of subsistence and other economic activities in the central-eastern Interior has shifted according to regional and global economic trends. If gold prices were high, mining increased; if furs were sought, then more people started trapping. Often there were no clear distinctions between people of different occupations. People incorporated any possible means of making a living into their lives, and this, in effect, meant that incomes were received piecemeal from mining, trapping, woodcutting, and, increasingly in modern times, seasonal wage labor, including crews that work on forest fires. Miners trapped, trappers mined, and shopkeepers got their moose as surely as anyone else. Hunting and fishing have provided, and still provide, many locals with their staple foods. Hunting and fishing have always involved relationships between hunters and their prey, though these are manifested and expressed differently between cultures.

The local indigenous relationship to fish and wildlife has always been, and continues to be, spiritual in nature, revolving around issues of respect and ritual behavior demonstrating this respect. Respect flows not only between hunter and prey but also and very importantly between both hunter and prey and the land. As the land provides for the people, the people owe respect and thankfulness back to the land, thereby completing the relationship through reciprocation. As noted by Elders who participated in this study, and others besides, the health of the land is a reflection of the health of its stewards—the people—and the well-being of the people is dependent on the well-being of the land. As the land (and water) and its expressions (through plants and animals, including humans) provide for material needs, those who receive provide spiritual awareness and respect back to the land and its expressions, acknowledging the gifts received and completing the circle of interdependency. As was intimated by Elders on multiple occasions, "We need the land, and the land needs us. Break this relationship and both will suffer." One of the most important cultural aspects of relationship to the land is language, which defines and is defined by the environment, and which reflects and is reflected by worldview.

Languages

Languages continue to clearly define ethnic boundaries, though the shared language is English and the majority of indigenous Alaskans use English as their first language. Elders especially, but also many others, continue to use their indigenous language in conversation, often interspersed among English words to provide additional details or information, and often focusing on concepts not readily expressible in English. The added details tend toward information regarding the land, its inhabitants (both human and otherwise), its conditions, or the weather. For example, Elders explained how they can express much detail in Hän or Gwich'in regarding moose: different words or word forms are used to express sex and age of a moose, and these are connected to identifiers that indicate that moose's activity at that time of year. Addition words use word variation (prefixes, suffixes) to indicate direction or weather information.

Though long suppressed by non-Native missionaries and government officials, particularly in education settings such as boarding schools, indigenous Alaska languages are currently experiencing a revival. The two languages spoken in this project's study area are Gwich'in and Hän (Hän is often referred to as Hän Gwich'in or Hän Hwëch'in, denoting its relatively close relation with Gwich'in). According to local estimations, there are today approximately 750 fluent Gwich'in speakers of a population of about 6,000 to 9,000 (US and Canada), while there are approximately ten to twenty fluent Hän speakers of a population of about 300 to 400 (US and Canada). Alaska Native languages are known for the detailed focus of vocabulary and grammar on land and weather features, as well as specifics on animal development, body parts, and behaviors.

The Setting, Its Resources, and Its Inhabitants: A Story of Relationships

The land is an enduring and changing symbol of identity for those who depend on its resources. For this reason, the land is often seen as sacred, as aware of its own conditions, and the nature of the land invariably affects the nature of its people. Therefore, a few words describing the geographical setting of the region can help to paint the picture of the land on which the histories of the people have unfolded, and of how these features helped to shape the local history as much as did the people who are the region's historical characters. As the land informs and shapes a culture in a dynamic way—in that a culture also identifies with and shapes a land—ethics of behavior emerge, including sharing and respect to enable sustainable, reciprocal sharing and balance through local "management" of living and nonliving resources. In fact, this management is in reality more of an issue of self-management than of resource management.

The term *management* is a culturally Western concept, and it is more accurate to describe Alaska Natives' decision-making processes concerning resources to be the outcome of maintaining balanced relationships with nonhuman entities. In other words, the resources are not seen as being owned or controlled by humans, but the interdependency that exists between humans and nonhumans necessitates respectful relations for sharing needs: humans provide for the spiritual needs of the nonhuman entities, who reciprocally provide for humans' material needs. These needs and expectations are learned simultaneously (and endlessly) through the traditional knowledge imparted by Elders and by *participating* in the formation and maintenance of relationships themselves. Such personal and intimate relationships provide for profound depths of knowledge about local conditions and enable sustainable survival in otherwise marginal environments.

Local, traditional, indigenous knowledge regarding the environment, and resource management issues that can be addressed by this knowledge, provide for a comprehensive understanding of the conditions in the region, including the well-being and location of caribou. Eagle residents, informed by the hunters and trappers on the land, consistently raise the issue of their limited access to caribou due to the heavy influx of out-of-town hunters who possess the means to harvest caribou from the Fortymile herd more efficiently and earlier than many Eagle residents. Often, the season is closed before the caribou arrive in the vicinity of Eagle Village and City (Koskey 2007, 15). As part of the Fortymile Caribou Harvest Management Plan, the Fortymile herd is closely tracked through the use of hunting reports, and while Fish and Wildlife management attempts to provide for all user groups, these reports neither cover the full scale of use nor are consistently accurate due to recall error. Other methods, such as aerial population counts, add information for management decisions, but only with the inclusion of local knowledge will this large-scale, top-down management be made more effective. Unifying multiple local management regimes under a statewide system has been informally suggested by various Alaska Native Elders across the state; local management would occur autonomously but in coordination with regional and statewide goals and principles, with cost and resource sharing being provided where needed.

By far, caribou hunters of the region report that the Fortymile herd was their main source of caribou (Koskey 2007, 138).[2] With such an influx of outside hunters and under conditions of nonlocal government management, much of the local traditional knowledge is unknown or disregarded, and so local conditions are largely out of the control of local hunters, trappers, and leaders. Very large numbers of nonlocals hunt the Fortymile herd and often use off-road vehicles or aircraft to access hunting areas that locals cannot afford; frequently, they leave behind the less-desirable parts of hunted caribou (Isaac Juneby, personal communication, February 2010).

---

2   The population of the Fortymile herd has fluctuated greatly over the years, from an estimated 200,000 in the 1920s to about 6,000 in 1973, with a recent estimated population of 50,000 (Mowry 2010c).

As with any government authority, regulations help or hinder subsistence activities, depending on the situation. This is a controversial issue for locals. State and federal regulations have hindered subsistence activities because a sport-hunting season has been opened, allowing harvest for sport use. Furthermore, regulations follow a bureaucratically approved calendar for hunting seasons that rarely takes into account the climatic situation. If the fall is warmer or arrives later than usual, it does not affect the regulation, but it does affect the behavior of the animal being harvested. The people of the area are not given much time to actually hunt, based on the regulation (Sanders 2009). Due to the repeated expression of dissatisfaction with out-of-town hunters, a special federal subsistence season has been added that allows subsistence hunters to hunt for caribou on federal lands at times other than the general hunt. Adjustments such as these have provided additional opportunity for residents of Eagle City, Eagle Village, Circle, and Central to be successful, and such opportunity is important in the rugged lands of the central-eastern Interior of Alaska. Nevertheless, it falls to the residents of these communities to keep up to date as to what their designation is, where all the surrounding federal land boundaries are, and who has jurisdiction over that land, as each agency has different regulations governing land use. This system places the onus on the hunter to self-educate regarding the regulations and one's own status under the law, which differs between state and federal regulations. Current federal designation of a subsistence hunter is a rural resident without respect to ethnicity. Further confusing the issue, different seasons with differing rules are provided by federal regulations in many places. Negotiating the complex regulations surrounding hunting, fishing, and trapping in the Interior's broken and rugged terrain has proven so difficult that some have either ceased these activities or perform them secretively to avoid harassment or prosecution.

Geography of the Central-Eastern Interior of Alaska

The central-eastern Interior is covered with mountains of moderate height and rolling forested hills almost everywhere. Being essentially irregular and broken plateau highlands, the central-eastern Interior is harsh even by Alaska standards, but due to the relationship that local people—both indigenous and nonindigenous Alaskans alike— have with the land, living on and from the land is possible. In some areas of Alaska—particularly in the west—rural populations are growing; in the Interior, some villages are experiencing population declines while others are relatively stable. Certainly, the nature of the relationships with the land varies between indigenous and nonindigenous populations. Each has heavily influenced the other, and through interviews during this project it became clear that there is much greater crossover of beliefs and values than is apparent at the surface. Though languages and cultures maintain the ethnic separation of indigenous and nonindigenous peoples, the environment brings both together through common economic activities ranging from subsistence to wage labor, from hunting-fishing-trapping to mineral extraction, and at the local level especially all are interdependently reliant on what the lands and waters of the region provide. Furthermore, Alaska Natives and non-Natives share common experiences of long-distance travel to reach places outside their community, whether on the Steese Highway, the Taylor Highway, or Yukon River, for visiting; obtaining supplies; reaching hunting, fishing, and trapping sites; attending funerals, potlatches, and weddings; and for aiding in community-wide disaster-relief efforts such as floods and fires.

The central-eastern Interior of Alaska is situated along the border of Canada's Yukon Territory, straddling the Yukon River and its nearby drainages and surrounding, usually mountainous lands. Though the mountains that dominate the landscape only occasionally exceed six thousand feet, they are very rugged and difficult to traverse. Other major watercourses in the region include the Charley River, the lower Tatonduk River, the lower Nation River, the lower Kandik River, the Seventymile River, Birch Creek, Coal Creek, Woodchopper Creek, and Washington Creek. Some call the 150 miles of the Yukon River from the Canadian border to the community of Circle the Upper Ramparts, referring to the often-steep chasms and canyons through which the Yukon flows.

As the Yukon reaches the vast Yukon Flats near Circle, the watercourses break into multiple braided channels that continue downriver to near Stevens Village at the western edge of the Yukon Flats. Beyond the

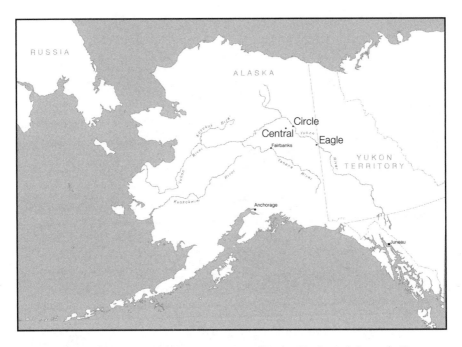

Figure 1. Map of Alaska with the communities of Eagle, Circle, and Central. (Courtesy of National Park Service)

Yukon Flats, the river's courses merge as it enters the Lower Ramparts. In much of the eastern Interior, deep, narrow, steep-walled valleys overlooked by rounded peaks in excess of five thousand feet characterize the land on either side. Flowing at an average rate of six to eight miles per hour, the Yukon broadens from almost half a mile wide at the border to nearly two miles wide at Circle (Ducker 1982, 8). The Tatonduk, Nation, and Kandik Rivers drain the surrounding Ogilvie Mountains (among others) from the northeast, while the Charley, Seventymile, and Fortymile Rivers drain the highlands—especially Glacier Mountain—from the west and south. The western reaches of the lands in the central-eastern Interior lie within the expansive Yukon-Tanana Uplands situated south of the Yukon Flats. The 4,000-to-5,000-foot peaks of this upland region constitute the White Mountains and the Crazy Mountains west of the community of Circle and are drained primarily by the Fortymile, Charley, and Seventymile Rivers, and by Beaver and Birch Creeks (both more

Figure 2. The Charley River at the "Rock Garden." (Courtesy of National Park Service)

Figure 3. Sharp ridges of exposed rocks in the Ogilvie Mountains in Yukon–Charley Rivers National Preserve. (Courtesy of National Park Service)

properly rivers). These waterways are well known for their sometimes-damaging floods.

As noted by Darbyshire and Associates (1990a), two of the natural hazards of the communities of Central, Circle, and Eagle have been flooding and erosion (caused mainly by the flooding). Some of the homes in the communities are located on or near the riverbanks, and many of the activities carried out by community members are in or on the area's waterways. After a long winter, when the snow starts to accumulates in September, the warmth of the spring sun causes rapid snowmelt. Due to the existence of permafrost and the frozen condition of the ground, the snowmelt does not penetrate the soil but runs off. The creeks usually overflow their banks, and then the rapid movement of ice scrapes along the banks, causing erosion; if the spring thaw is rapid enough, it can cause the creeks and rivers to carve new channels. Summer thundershowers can also cause the water flow to increase dramatically. As described by a local resident, "It is not unusual, in the course of an ordinary summer thunderstorm, to have the Birch and its tributaries rise several feet in less than an hour, threatening any activities along the banks and cutting transportation routes until the water level drops" (Oakes 1983, 3). Another account mirrors this description:

> Riverbank erosion is a natural process that occurs as a river evolves and grades its course. Meandering rivers move back and forth across flood plains and occasionally extend the plain laterally. Erosion occurs at the outside bank of bends or curves where running water undercuts bank sediments, causing overhang, eventual collapse and a renewal of the process. The rate of erosion depends on the type of sediment in banks, wave action and vegetative cover and is usually most severe during times of high, rapid water at break-up or during storm-related floods. (Darbyshire and Associates 1990a)

But destructive flooding is a relatively rare occurrence, and the rivers are the habitat of the primary food source of the region: fish. Local fish include, from late spring to early fall, multiple species of salmon, including dog (or chum) salmon, king (or chinook) salmon, and silver (or coho) salmon. There are also many species of whitefish that overwinter in the region's rivers. In addition to these, other fish are commonly found throughout the area, including sheefish, northern pike, Arctic grayling, longnose sucker, burbot, and Arctic lamprey (Marcus et al. 2004, 25). Residents depend heavily on fish for subsistence, particularly salmon on the Yukon and whitefish, pike, and grayling in smaller watercourses. Salmon fishing by local residents occurs primarily on the Yukon River at Eagle and Circle, although a few reported fishing at the Chitina River, a tributary of the Copper River, in the Wrangell–St. Elias Mountains to the south of the Tanana Valley (Koskey 2007, 13–14). There are also several fish camps along the Yukon between Circle and Eagle.

The area's rough topography allows for regional variation in weather conditions, and as in other parts of Interior Alaska, valleys tend to be colder—sometimes much more so—than highland areas. This is due to temperature inversions, where the colder, heavier air descends to lower elevations and the lighter, warmer air ascends to higher elevations. The more frequent and stronger winds of the higher elevations can at times

Figure 4. Little Black River Hills overlooking plain with thermokarst lakes. (Courtesy of National Park Service)

reverse this trend, and windchill factors can eliminate the warmth at higher elevations caused by inversions. Throughout the region, permafrost is frequent, though from four to fifteen inches of permafrost melts each summer. Most of this refreezes in the fall and winter, though permanent permafrost melting has been observed throughout Alaska for a few decades. Permafrost melting leaves very visible traces through thermokarst, which is a land surface cavity that forms as permafrost thaws, often characterized by sinkholes and tussocks. For example, the heat trapped by the roadbed led to the formation of a thermokarst, creating a sinkhole that led to the collapse of the road.

More typically, however, thermokarst forms in low-lying areas as the temperature of the land's surface increases. This is demonstrated in figure 4, which shows wet terraces with thermokarst lakes in the region of the Little Black River Hills in the Yukon–Charley Rivers National Preserve. As observed by Jorgenson (2001), "The degradation of permafrost can lead to large changes in ecosystems, land use and infrastructure that rely on permafrost for a foundation." In addition to thawing caused by warming air temperatures, the three principal causes of permafrost thawing are low snow cover, wildfires, and groundwater movement (Jorgenson 2001, 573).

Forest fires, too, are linked to climate change (see Flannigan et al. 2000 for a discussion of previous research on this subject). Flannigan et al. review evidence that fire weather severity in the circumpolar North, including Alaska, has increased considerably over the past few decades. They also report that data show that "[a]s a first guess we would expect increases in area burned for the United States of 25–50% by the middle of the 21st century with most of the increases occurring in Alaska and the southeastern United States" (Jorgenson 2001, 226).

Within these conditions of high variability, both humans and the greater environment are finding adaptation to be increasingly difficult. As one of the coldest and driest portions of Alaska, together with its ever-rugged landforms and low populations, the central-eastern Interior can be a difficult place to survive for those unfamiliar with the land and climate. While some capacities for survival are based on the accumulation of local and indigenous knowledge, introduced technologies such as rifles, boat motors, and other manufactured goods also help in survival and lessen the risks involved in living in such a rich yet harsh environment. Again, a blending of cultural traditions and technological innovations demonstrate the importance of local and indigenous knowledge that now is shared between indigenous and settler populations, and a mutually strengthening interdependence is evident.

Summary

The coming together of these streams of knowledge—one based on deep and intimate relationships with the land and its inhabitants, the other based on technological innovation and machine-based knowledge traditions—makes the central-eastern Interior of Alaska more easily and more comfortably inhabitable for both indigenous and settler peoples. The rise and success of this shared experience of life on the land that includes both indigenous people and settlers is the focus of this ethnohistory. As a central focus of this work, Hän Hwëch'in Elder Isaac Juneby provides the opening firsthand account of life in the central-eastern Interior of Alaska in a time of rapid change. Following Isaac's perspective on his local and personal history is a description of the historical and culture-defining gold mining in the Circle Mining District, located on the other, western side of the Yukon–Charley Rivers National Preserve that separates Eagle from Circle and Central.

The fundamental theme of this people's history is one of cooperation and sharing, a consequent rise of cross-cultural interdependency, and a reliance on multiple traditions of knowledge—crossing the boundaries of one's tradition and forging ways of life. These are processes that are ongoing and accelerating locally, nationally, and internationally, and these processes lead to often-difficult periods of culture change. By understanding the origins, causes, and consequences of this change—here in the form of an accessible ethnohistory—the stresses that invariably accompany such change can be identified, and appropriate and adequate mitigations can be put in place. When developed with respect, cultural appropriateness, and equality of inclusion of all affected groups, effective reactions to changes can be achieved in terms of community development, resource management, and research.

The three communities in this study—Eagle, Circle, and Central— possess local histories that include ongoing traditions of cross-cultural sharing and culture change. More so than any other single activity, all three communities have been greatly affected by gold-mining activities, and one—Central—essentially exists as a direct result of gold mining. For this reason, each community's history includes important influences from gold miners and their activities, and this gold-mining history has been inexorably intertwined with all other historical strands since its advent. Two other activities also permeate other historical concerns in the communities: fur trapping for commercial markets, which continues to the present, and timber cutting, which ceased on a large scale with the demise of wood-and-steam-powered engines used by mining equipment and the riverboats, usually called sternwheelers. Here are the stories of the people of Eagle, Central, and Circle that, when blended with archival information, form the ethnohistory of Alaska's central-eastern Interior, linked by the Yukon River, gold mining, and long-shared cultural connections and forming a multicultural, multiple-community, interconnected self-sufficiency.

Isaac Juneby, introduced at the beginning of this chapter, lived to participate in most of these activities, combining his life experience and accumulated local, traditional, indigenous knowledge with wage labor work to become a leader among his Hän Hwëch'in people. In addition to always stressing the importance of formal education, Isaac spoke of the continuing importance of traditional knowledge—even concerning identity, as he ended his speech:

> So, traditional knowledge should not be overlooked, discounted, in addressing cultural resource management simply because it is not written down. Traditional knowledge is the property of the people who possess it. Traditional knowledge is respected, used, and passed on. Traditional knowledge also provides the Alaska Natives with an understanding of who they are. And that's the best way I could try to explain that, is when we talk about land, you hear people say they tie themselves back to the land. That's what they mean right there. It is important to understand that the need for including traditional knowledge is in the best interest in the management of our resources. I hope that in the future when we review some of the management plans, GMP [General Management Plan], just any kind of a plan, any research, even an SOP [standard operating procedure], that we consider some of this traditional knowledge to use it. It is understood that the separation of culture and nature is a Western concept and not necessarily how the universe is viewed by Natives. So in closing, I would like to say that I hope that I have given you my perspective on what traditional knowledge is. And I tried to explain it within the best way... to make it simple... Thank you for giving me the opportunity.

TWO

A Story of Eagle, Alaska

EAGLE, ALASKA, INCLUDES two communities located a few miles from one another: Eagle City and Eagle Village. Eagle City is populated by mostly non-Native settlers and has a population of approximately eighty to ninety (Alaska Department of Commerce, Community and Economic Development [ADCCED], US census population, 2010). Eagle Village is predominantly Hän Athabascan (Dené) and has approximately sixty to seventy residents (ADCCED, 2010), though many with residences in Eagle Village also live temporarily or permanently in Fairbanks or other population centers. Therefore, the combined population of Eagle fluctuates between approximately 140 and 160, rising in the spring and summer and falling in the autumn and winter. Eagle is reached by a summer road (unplowed in winter) known as the Taylor Highway that connects south to the Alaska Highway at Tetlin Junction and southeast to Dawson, Yukon Territory, via the Top of the World Highway.

Since the arrival of Americans and other nonlocals in the area in the late nineteenth century, the population of Eagle has been ethnically mixed. Due to the early presence of Fort Egbert and the famous Third Judicial District court of Judge James Wickersham, the early history of Eagle is well documented (Wickersham 1938). But before the establishment of the fort and Wickersham's court, the long-present indigenous Athabascan

(Dené) people interacted with gold prospectors who had entered the region in the late nineteenth century. The local and regional indigenous Alaskans are the Hän Hwëch'in (usually referred to simply as Hän), who have lived in and around the Eagle area for countless generations. Given that history, this portion of the ethnohistory focuses on the Hän, though the importance of the settlers' role is also discussed.

Cultural exchange and economic interdependence began with the arrival of the first American explorers, trappers, and miners in the period following the US Civil War. Most of the new arrivals found themselves in very unfamiliar and difficult territory, and most looked to the local Hän to learn how to survive in this cold and rugged land. The story of the Hän, then, is primary to a story of Eagle, and in the case of Eagle, much of the more recent history is told through the eyes of Isaac Juneby, introduced at the beginning of this text, who was one of the principal participants in providing access to and compiling the information for the Eagle portion of this ethnohistorical work. Isaac's life story provides an example of the sharing of traditions and increasing interdependency that has arisen throughout Alaska as cultures meet, merge, and are redefined.

Before discussing the communities of Eagle[1] through the lens of Isaac Juneby, a brief overview of the area is in order. In precontact and early postcontact times, the Hän Hwëch'in people practiced the most widespread culture on the stretch of the Yukon River between the present-day towns of Dawson (Hän: *Tr'ochëk*) and Eagle (Hän: *Tthee T'äwdlenn*), continuing toward the Gwichyaa Gwich'in of Circle and surrounding regions (Slobodin 1963). Hän culture, like all cultures, developed hand-in-hand with the land itself, and the precontact Hän were seminomadic hunter-gatherer-fishers who derived much of their food from the yearly migrations of caribou and from various subspecies of salmon that run up the Yukon River and its tributaries. Now, in the early years of the twenty-first century, the lands between Eagle Village, Dawson, and Moosehide (3.1 miles downriver from Dawson/*Tr'ochëk*) are the hubs of Hän culture. Hän culture has undergone tremendous

---

1   Eagle is colloquially called the City and the Village, in which dwell, respectively, most of the settlers and most of the Hän.

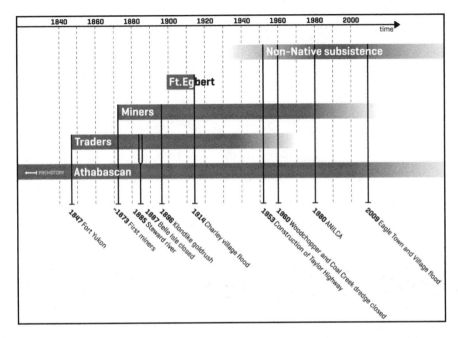

Figure 5. Timeline of events in the central-eastern Interior of Alaska. (By Heikki Lotvonen)

changes since early contact and the gold rushes of the mid- to late nineteenth century. The Hän in Yukon Territory experienced contact and culture change earlier than many interior Athabascan groups due to their proximity to the goldfields. Beginning with a trickle of outsiders with the Forty Mile gold strike (1892), this migration turned into a steady stream of newcomers with the Birch Creek strikes (1893) and ballooned into a veritable flood of settlers with the advent of the Klondike gold rush. In the years of contact between Hän and settlers before the gold rushes, the Hän were able to control the local situation regarding contact, culture change, and language use, but with the arrival of miners by the thousands, this control was compromised. In fact, many miners and trappers traveling from the Klondike had previously moved into and through the Peel River drainage, where contact with the Tetlit Gwich'in led to a measles epidemic (Slobodin 1981), greatly reducing the population and its control over its well-being—a situation to be endured next by the Hän. Livelihoods and well-being began to rapidly change among the Hän from the period beginning in the late nineteenth century into the twentieth century and continuing to the present.

Isaac Juneby's Story and the Communities of Eagle

Elder Isaac Juneby was an invaluable project partner in the creation of this ethnohistory. A lifelong resident of Eagle Village, Isaac was an integral part of the communities of Eagle Village and Eagle City. He worked to bridge the cultural differences between his Hän people and outsiders who have come to call Alaska home. In these efforts, Isaac was involved in local and regional government affairs, the school board, and projects such as this ethnohistory. Isaac's life history and the history of his family illustrate the changes that have occurred in the lives of Hän people.

Isaac was comfortable and confident in local and cross-cultural situations, attracting notice, and the older he became, the more active he was in his community. With both locals and outsiders Isaac was willing to share memories and knowledge of the times of his youth and beyond, much of it gained from his Elders of earlier generations. Isaac did not know much about his family's origins, but he did share his knowledge on the seminomadic lifeways of his people, particularly before World War II, and his own considerable and comprehensive personal knowledge of Hän history and culture.

Juneby Family Background

Isaac's grandparents were children at the time of the Klondike gold rush (1896–1899) and the establishment of Fort Egbert (1899–1911) in Eagle. His great-grandparents would have been children in 1874, when the first permanent structure—the log trading post known as Belle Isle—was established at what is today Eagle. From the time of his own childhood, Isaac listened to the stories of his parents, grandparents, and great-grandparents, who passed down their firsthand memories of historical events and culture change in the region through oral history. He was ever eager to share these stories with anyone interested.

Like many other Elders but even more so, Isaac was able to take these stories of his people's past and put them in a context of culture change. The reason for this was Isaac's advantageous upbringing, wherein he was largely isolated from non-Hän peoples in his day-to-day life since his father and family lived and worked at woodcutting camps away from Eagle. In these settings, traditional stories were frequently told alongside more recent accounts from living memory. More than three generations of historical accounts were relayed to Isaac during and after the time he dwelled at the woodcutting camps, and when he moved back to Eagle permanently he could readily see the changes affecting his people. Isaac witnessed the full settling of his formerly seminomadic people in villages and the gradual loss of their Hän language as they adopted Anglo-American lifeways. This occurred in large part during and following his youth due to government requirements that children attend school, which was largely accomplished through boarding schools.

While at boarding schools, youth were removed from their traditional cultures and taught English and Anglo-American lifeways and values. This often led to rapid assimilation[2] and created a cultural and linguistic "break" between older and younger generations. Due to his relative isolation in his youth, Isaac retained his Hän language and culture more so than most others from his generation. Because of this, Isaac was ideally suited to be the local historian that he was, and through his life he served as a "cultural bridge" between the Hän and the settlers, and between the past and the present. Isaac understood and, when not in boarding school, participated in the subsistence lifeways of his ancestors, yet he also took part in the happenings of the larger world, including wage employment and military service. From the seasonal round of the subsistence cycle to the time clock of wage labor, Isaac participated in and gained experiences of both lifeways.

---

2   *Assimilation* is the process by which a culture of a society is replaced by the culture of another society; the process can be forced (as in early Alaska under the Russians, and later under the Americans) or voluntary.

The Hän Seasonal Round

The subsistence economy traditionally used by the Hän was a reflection of their knowledge of the lands and waters of their region, as well as of the inhabitants of these lands and waters. Economy being only one aspect of subsistence, the seasonal round included all the activities necessary for economic provision and, at least in most times, for survival. The complexity of the natural world is never fully predictable, however, and though all seasons provided at least minimal necessary resources, scarcity and starvation would occasionally occur. The seasonal round is the summary of life activities that are inextricably linked to form a tradition of subsistence that when practiced as a whole could provide great resilience and sustainability to a community. Though the conditions of the modern world have led to the modification or abandonment of some subsistence practices, a great many persist to the present, and many modern traditions derive from older subsistence traditions.

Now, with the blending of older and newer cultural practices, the seasonal round persists as a tradition that continues to inform Alaska Natives about the world around them and when to expect the environmental changes that repeat through the seasonal cycle as indicated by locally recognized natural indicators. For example, Isaac explained that when a particular patch of snow melted on the bluffs overlooking the Yukon River in Eagle, the king salmon (chinook) would soon arrive, and so they usually do. Isaac explained that this and similar knowledge was passed to him by his father and uncles, and this particular example also illustrates the conditions of local indigenous knowledge regarding subsistence activities and the seasonal round. In recent times, due to rapid climate change in Alaska, these natural indicators sometimes no longer consistently apply, limiting their practical applicability, but these natural indicators are only a fraction of the persistent cultural knowledge needed to understand and maintain the seasonal round, whether in earlier or more contemporary forms.

Often, the cultural traditions of the seasonal round are the most deeply established and longest enduring, elucidating material, spiritual, and cosmological knowledge and beliefs. Isaac experienced some of the Hän seasonal round in his lifetime, though by the time of his childhood in the 1940s, the traditional seasonal round was already changing to meet contemporary economic needs and opportunities. Isaac explained the seasonal round from the perspective of his parents and grandparents. The Hän who comprised the band that included Isaac's parents (as children) and grandparents traveled from one place to another over the course of the year in pursuit of changing yet seasonal natural resources, including both plants and animals. The Hän migration pattern started in the vicinity of Eagle and continued south to Ketchumstuk (near the present-day settlement of Chicken), where they remained during the winter. In the summer they returned to the lakes and the rivers of the region, primarily for fishing. The Hän then traveled southwest to Mansfield Lake (adjacent to present-day Tanacross) and from there to Tetlin (to the southeast of Mansfield Lake) and on to the White River in today's Yukon Territory. They then floated the White River to the Yukon River down to the vicinity of present-day Dawson and Moosehide, and later continued downriver (on the Yukon) to the vicinity of present-day Eagle, where they fished and hunted until fall, when the cycle began again. This annual cycle of migration was very familiar to Isaac, and though he did not follow it himself (nor did anyone during his lifetime), his familiarity came from the traditional knowledge he gained from his elders.

Isaac noted that there were three different villages in the area during his youth in the 1940s. His family, for example, had relatives in a place that they called Charley Village, after Chief Charley, which was located at the mouth of the Kandik River. Isaac and Chief Charley are from the same people but of a different clan. One of the main dwelling places was in the vicinity of present-day Eagle, where Isaac was born, though they stayed quite a while at each place in the yearly cycle. The third Hän settlement was Moosehide Village on the Canadian side, where Isaac also has relatives (Juneby 2010).

This seasonal round was based on the deep traditional knowledge the Hän had accumulated over generations, and it proved to be both a sustainable and resilient cultural adaptation to the needs and demands of the people and the place. The seasonal round movement was still very much in place when the first outsiders, who were mostly fur trappers and traders, arrived in the region. These events occurred before Isaac was born.

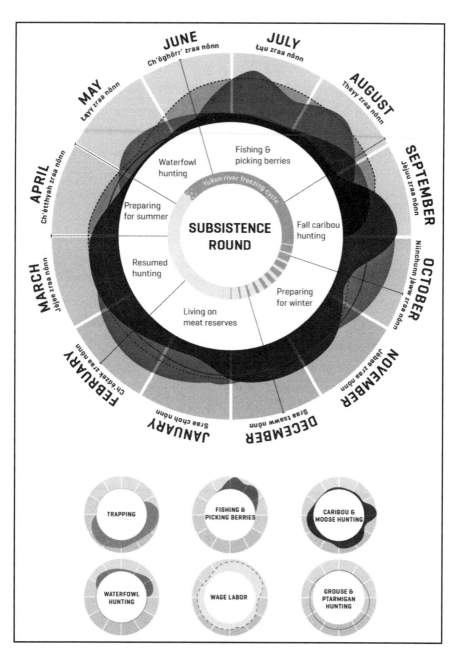

Figure 6. Subsistence round of the Hän with English and Hän months. (By Heikki Lotvonen)

Indigenous hunter-trappers traded furs with settlers and also provided them with provisions such as meat and sometimes acted as guides.

Early Contacts and Trade Between the Hän and Settlers

The earliest written account concerning contact with the Hän people starts with the journals of Alexander Hunter Murray. He worked for Hudson's Bay Company and built the first trading post—Fort Yukon—near Hän territory in 1847. According to the Dawson Indian Band, "Murray was apprehensive about the Hän, who were very angry at the construction of a fort so close to their territory" (Kosuta 1988, 8), but their frightening and aggressive ways seemed also to fascinate Murray, who often wrote about his encounters with the Hän people:

> [W]e were a different people from the Russians and not so easily frightened, we were always prepared against enemies, we did not come here to give away our goods for nothing, but they [the Hän] would be well paid for what they bought, and if they came as friends they would always be well treated. After some more quibbling they professed to be our friends… (Murray 1910, 61)

Though the trading post was also indisputably a fort, trade was the primary interest and the fort itself was only used for trade and to secure trade goods within.

Early traders noticed that the Natives were not strangers to Western manufactured goods. The Hän were already familiar with foreign products, due to trade routes that indirectly and directly connected them to Russian traders, and with Native goods from other bands, in an extensive network (Webb 1985, 47; Reynolds and Jordan 1983, 38, citing Hall 1976, 349). Through this trade the Hän acquired items such as dentalium shells, obsidian, and walrus-hide babiche, in addition to Western trade goods such as tea or coffee, dry goods, firearms and ammunition, tobacco, and sometimes sweets or alcohol (Griffin 1988, 33). Isaac said that his own grandfather traded furs for these items, as did his earlier ancestors throughout the Hän regions.

Because of connections with indigenous peoples and cohabitation on the lands, the early trading companies competed not only with each other but also with the Native trade networks. According to Anglican missionary Richard J. Bowen, who wrote his observations (1898–1903) about trading between the Hän people and bands of the Ketchumstuk area, he was not allowed to participate in trading but was obliged to remain at the camp. Bowen speculated that the reason for this was that the Hän didn't want to jeopardize their monopoly by letting Ketchumstuk people meet non-Native traders (Mishler and Simeone 2004, 7).

In times of early trading, the Native people remained highly independent, enjoying Western manufactured goods but not relying on them. According to the journals of Alexander Hunter Murray, at first the most-wanted items were beads and guns (though this has been challenged by local archaeological investigations that show trade items such as beads were not important in relation to other items of material culture) (Sanders 2011). Interestingly, cloth items that the traders wanted to exchange for furs were not accepted by the Native people, who felt that their own clothes were superior in beauty and durability (Murray 1910, 56). Murray also observed that "comparatively little of their [Native people's] time is devoted to hunting furs, they talk as if they could get what they wanted at any time" (Murray 1910, 89). This suggests, as many secondary sources also conclude, that the people maintained their independence during the early contact times and that they did not rush into the world of Western economies but rather utilized whatever tools made life easier. Rapid change, however, came with the gold rushes of the era, including the Forty Mile (1892) and then the Birch Creek (1893) strikes that led to the establishment of Circle and Central and, finally, the most famous: the Klondike (1896), which involved the Hän from the beginning.

The Influences and Consequences of Gold

The discovery of gold in the heart of the Hän homeland had a lasting effect on Hän culture as the dramatic influx of miners caused significant changes in the economies, the demographics, and ultimately the landscape itself. After some smaller gold finds in the Forty Mile country and the Circle Mining District—most notably by Jack McQuesten in 1892—and elsewhere, very promising amounts of gold were found in the Klondike River in Canada, resulting in a gold rush that began in August of 1896. Fredrick Fairweather Flewelling, a young missionary from the Anglican Church, observed the atmosphere and the changes that happened during the years he spent as a missionary in the area. He left an already-established mission at the Fortymile River and traveled to the Klondike region to "take care of the souls there." He writes:

October 31st [1896] Klondick. Early in September there was great excitement among the miners, gold creeks having been found on the Klondick River about fifty miles above F. Mile on the Yukon, and all were rushing up here to stake claims. (Flewelling 1898)

After the winter, only six months later, he writes in a journal entry:

Thlondick [*sic*], May 29th [1897]. We reached here last night but could hardly recognize the old place because of so many tents. Five or six hundred men have already come in this spring and their tents are pitched everywhere. (Flewelling 1898)

The population of Dawson City, which was established near the Klondike River and goldfields, was booming as the general excitement drew thousands of people into the country, some poorly equipped and unprepared, others fully capable of living the hard life of a prospector. Isaac Juneby would sometimes refer directly to these times, when his own grandparents were young adults. By recounting their stories of life in and around Eagle, and the accompanying changes at the turn of the twentieth century, Isaac provided information from his grandparents' stories, helping to create some of the ethnohistorical accounts throughout this portion of this study.

Lifestyle changes increased with the influx of outsiders, one of the first consequences being that the non-Native people took over many viable sites, such as fish camps, that were traditionally utilized by Hän people, forcing them to relocate their traditional subsistence use areas and

Figure 7. Moosehide, Yukon Territory, a Hän village upriver from Eagle, circa 1910. (Archives, University of Alaska Fairbanks, Rivenburg Collection, USUAFV5-75, UAF-1994-70-333)

settlements. Changes were major, especially in the Klondike. New settlements quickly appeared, and existing ones experienced large and rapid population growth, though few retained these larger populations for long, especially once the gold was mostly discovered and mined out.

One such place was Dawson City, founded on the mouth of the Klondike River in an area that was the traditional land of the easternmost Hän band, the Trondek Hwëch'in, whose old village used to be in Nuklako, located thirteen miles below the Klondike River (Webb 1977, 11). According to oral histories, the mouth of the Klondike River was an ancient fishing site and a village of the Tr'ondëk Hwëch'in people. The booming growth of Dawson and Klondike City (which was commonly called Lousetown), forced the Hän people to relocate their village to a site known as Moosehide, a place with which Isaac and his family were very familiar.

The establishment of Eagle and Circle, and later Central, stems from the migrations of the gold rush era. According to Judge James

Figure 8. Local family at Forty Mile, near Eagle, ca. 1899, with dogsled and tent, next to moss-roofed house. (University of Washington Libraries, Special Collections, Eric A. Hegg, photographer, NA2450)

Wickersham, in 1895 there were already 4,500 miners in the newly found goldfields near the communities of Circle and Eagle. The establishment of towns and rapid population growth were radical changes for the area, which had been so sparsely populated ten years earlier. According to oral histories, the town of Eagle was built on the site of an old Hän settlement, and below the graveyard, which was inundated in the destructive flood of 2009, was Johnny's Village (Shinkwin 1976, 1978; Paul and Ridley 1991; Juneby 2010). Isaac's father, Willie Juneby, also recalled in an oral history interview with Reggie Sobel that the Hän summer camp and a cemetery used to be by Eagle Bluff, but the village was moved as requested by the soldiers of Fort Egbert. Willie recalls that when he was a boy, in the early 1900s, all the cabins in the village were fairly new due to the influx of gold miners and their families (Juneby 1980).

Figure 9. Hän Athabascan log cabin under construction at the village of Eagle, Alaska, early twentieth century. (Courtesy of the Archives of the Episcopal Church)

The Klondike gold rush was over quite suddenly, as the miners who had not found their fortunes heard about other promising goldfields and left nearly as quickly as they had come. News from Nome in 1899, and later from the lower Tanana Valley rush in 1902, nearly emptied the creeks, leaving behind ghost towns such as Nation and Star City that had been so densely populated that they had their own post offices. Despite the gold rushes to other places, small populations of stubborn miners continued working on their claims and supporting the few communities that survived when fortune seekers deserted the area. According to local accounts, the central-eastern Interior became quieter, but the communities of Eagle and Circle continued to thrive due to their important locations along the Yukon River, which served in many ways as a highway into the interior of Alaska.

Connections Between Local History and Isaac Juneby's Life History

Isaac explained that before his time, the leader of a village was a chief (though he emphasizes that this is an English word that has no direct equivalent in Hän), advised by his council. Chiefs had to be knowledgeable in their own culture's ways, and they were chosen based on their character and selfless dedication to their community, with a focus on benevolent behaviors. Each had to know about his culture and way of life and be well respected. Chiefs were understood to be wise and respected people, and they were never denigrated socially or personally. Chief Charley (for whom Charley's Village was named, and sometimes spelled Charlie) and Chief Isaac were known to be shrewd men in their own ways, and they did not want their people to mix with other people. As a result, Isaac explained, the Hän people never made any trouble with the settlers. Once contact was made, the Hän people and the settlers got along due to a need for interdependence, and they taught each other knowledge and skills as needed, including hunting; tanning; fishing; gathering; traditional medicine; food preservation; use and maintenance of guns, machinery, and other tools; and, inevitably in the colonial context, English, Christianity, and the laws of the United States. Among the Hän, most notably, there was an early change in material culture and a later, more gradual change in other cultural traditions, including kinship reckoning (due to intermarriage) and spirituality (due to missionizing).

According to Richard Caulfield (1979), Hän material culture had already changed significantly by the time of the gold rush, increasing Hän people's reliance on Western goods. At the same time, the traders' interests had shifted from furs to gold. Hän people had become accustomed to having certain manufactured products, such as guns and ammunition, matches, cotton, and various kinds of non-Native foods; but, because furs were not as valuable a trade item as gold, the Native people lost their upper hand and had to trade on terms that were not necessarily as favorable as they had been earlier. As a consequence, they did not have a say in coming changes when traders moved their trading posts into newly established mining towns instead of staying in locations that were favorable for the Hän (Mishler and Simeone 2004, 8; Webb 1977, 49–50).

In spite of the declining value of trade from the indigenous perspective, the popularity of Western goods continued and even increased. In the latter years of the nineteenth century clothing, especially, came into use among the Hän (and others), as is evident in photographs of the time (Simeone 2007). In a 2010 interview, Isaac said that many of the trade items "were cheap" and some of the trade goods replaced the goods that were already used. Suddenly, fabric became available, and it was even cheaper than moose skin. The perception of the value of industrial items greatly influenced how things changed, Isaac recounted, including a drive for cash to acquire manufactured goods that led many into wage labor. People looked for cheaper goods that could serve the same purpose as formerly used items. The skins that the Hän wore were labor intensive to make, unlike the new materials that could be acquired by trade. Much of this trade was directed at the fastest-growing segment of settlers—the miners—who, like the Native people, would travel to trading posts. Trading posts provided additional, and very influential, places to interact and share information between the Hän and the settlers. Out on the land, however, and particularly along the rivers, miners' activities increasingly disrupted the lives of indigenous peoples through the overharvest of animals, settlement and mining on lands previously used by Alaska Natives, and polluting of streams (whether temporarily or permanently). In addition to these disruptions, other difficult and sometimes-oppressive changes arrived with missionaries and government officials; interaction with these soon led to increasing dependence that, when coupled with dependence on traders for access to outside goods (foods, manufactured items), led to rapid cultural changes.

As a result of the increasing non-Native population, the creeks of the Hän homeland were suddenly full of miners and prospectors who competed with the Hän for the same natural resources. The mining activities disturbed wildlife populations, which migrated farther from the gold-bearing creeks (Mishler and Simeone 2004, 13–14). This was especially problematic in Dawson. According to Tappan Adney (1898, 963),

> The Indians have been hunting all winter and killed large numbers [of moose]. The miners are driving them further away from Dawson, but almost every day come reports of moose killed on Bonanza, Hunker, etc.

These Hän hunters were hired by prospectors and others to supply wild meat, or they traded meat obtained independently for outside goods. Soon, wildlife populations became severely depleted, and the animals moved to other areas, forcing the Hän to travel farther on their hunting trips (Dobrowolsky 2008, 42). Competition over resources became unsustainable as many miners lacked adequate supplies from the outside and had to buy wild meat from the Native hunters, or start hunting themselves, to supplement their food base (Caulfield 1979, 10). Some settlers and miners had very wasteful hunting practices, and they shot animals such as caribou and moose without ever intending to utilize all the meat or hides. This led to complaints from Hän leaders, namely Chief Isaac of Moosehide, who, as reported by the *Dawson Daily News* in 1911, publicly complained about the hunting practices of newcomers (Mishler and Simeone 2004, 16–17; Dobrowolsky 2008, 42):

All Yukon belong to my papas. All Klondike belong my people. Long time all mine. Hills all mine, caribou all mine, moose all mine, rabbits all mine, gold all mine. White man come and take all my gold. Take millions, take more hundreds fifty millions, and blow 'em in Seattle. Now Moosehide Injun want Christmas. Game is gone. White man kills all moose and caribou near Dawson… Moosehides hunt up Klondike, up Sixtymile, up Twentymile, but game is all gone. White man kill all.

This is a complaint that continues, in some cases, to be applicable to the present as populations in rural areas increase, or at least fluctuate.

The population influx to towns and creeks led the Native peoples to find themselves a minority in their own homelands, and non-Native presence had dire consequences on Hän culture. During this period, Alaska Natives were segregated and discriminated against, the legacy of which remains in the form of separate settler and indigenous communities in some villages. According to Isaac and other sources, the Hän of the Dawson area lost a great deal during the time of forced assimilation, including language, songs, dances, and potlatches. As the story goes, in the early 1900s, Chief Isaac, the leader of Dawson Indian band, traveled to the Tanacross area near Tok and told the people there "they [missionaries] took all our drums and songs away from us." He brought some songs and some drums to the town of Tok for safekeeping. At the time, missionaries had outlawed Native singing and dancing as being "heathen." Isaac Juneby tells that, years later, when singing and dancing were not suppressed by the government, the Tanacross people came back and returned the songs. The Dawson Hän were fortunate to have Laura Salmon from Tok to show them some of the traditional ways Chief Isaac had brought them, and thus they achieved a revival. Now they have reestablished drumming and dancing; they have a band, dance group, and singing group; and they practice regularly. Today, this revitalization is occurring throughout indigenous Alaska and Yukon after decades of openly stated policies of assimilation by national and regional governments, partly accomplished through required boarding schools, where indigenous languages and cultures were suppressed. Isaac explained that both governments (in Alaska and the Yukon) were aligned against the Native cultures, and this is one of the reasons why many of the traditional ways and even values were lost. This exacerbated the influence of Christian missionaries, who brought and promoted different values and worldviews, and who actively preached against indigenous spiritual beliefs and practices. Described in detail above, these processes of assimilation began with the arrival of gold miners in the Forty Mile country of the central-eastern Interior of Alaska, then soon after in the Klondike country (from the very late nineteenth century into the early twentieth century).

Economic Considerations of Cross-Cultural Contact and Culture Change in the Eagle Area

Native peoples' increasing familiarization with Western commerce, alongside the declining population of wild animals, led to their enmeshment in the global economy—resulting in an increasing need for the money that made store-bought goods and supplies available (Mishler and Simeone 2003, 14). At the same time, the expanding population of nonlocal people also created new economic opportunities for the Native people and sped up the changes in their lifeways. Willie Juneby (Isaac's father) tells that his own father cut wood in wintertime, trapped, and snared ptarmigan that he sold to the store in town, making ends meet for his family (Juneby 1980). Adeline Juneby-Potts of Eagle Village, Isaac's sister, writes, describing the employment situation of the mid-twentieth century,

> During the winters, most of the men would trap and then try to find some seasonal work the other parts of the year. Whether it was fire-fighting, road commission or working at the gold mines, it was a paying job and they could prepare for the long dark winters that lay ahead. (Juneby-Potts 1993, 31)

Logging

Usually, wage labor is seasonal, and seasonal employment is supplemented with subsistence activities, fishing, hunting, and trapping. In earlier times, wages could be earned by working at wood-cutting lots—referred to locally as logging camps—cutting timber and processing it for use in steam-driven engines, particularly the sternwheelers. One of the important logging camps that employed many Eagle Village men was Heine Miller's operation on Wood Island, situated downriver from Eagle at the mouth of the Tatonduk Creek. According to Matthew Malcolm, the locale may have gotten its name from an incident in 1937 in which a couple of the Eagle Village men survived an ice-breakup flood by climbing into a tree. They had to wait in the tree for a day and a half for the water level to drop enough so that they were able to cross the river and hike to the safety of Miller Camp (Malcolm 1991).

In addition to cutting wood, the Native people also worked on the steamboats because they often were experts of river navigation, and their skills were needed in negotiating the steamboats safely through difficult places (Malcolm 1991; Paul 1993). Oral historian William Schneider interviewed Matthew Malcolm:

> Eighty-two-year-old Matthew Malcolm from Eagle Village recalls that he got through the sixth or seventh grade but missed a lot of school because his family needed to make money. This meant cutting wood

for the steamboats at a camp on the Yukon River, five or six miles below Miller's place at Sheep Creek. He grew up with a few months of schooling a year but also a lot of time out in the woods working (pers. comm., November 20, 2008). His story is fairly typical. (Schneider 2012, 41)

Trapping

Other families found their main source of income from trapping. Hän elders interviewed in the 1990s still remember from their childhood how entire families moved to traplines for the winter, returning to camps and villages for Christmas. After Christmas celebrations, they continued trapping until spring (Malcolm 1991; Paul 1993). This changed when the school opened and parents were legally obliged to place their children in these schools, an act that would eventually lead to the end of seminomadism. Matthew Malcolm's oral history interview illustrates this change: at first, the entire family participated in the winter trapping trips, but later on, only the men went away for four to five months while the women stayed at Eagle, where the children went to school (Malcolm 1991; cf. Mishler and Simeone 2004, 57).

The United States–Canada Border

In response to seminomadism, administrative actions were taken to enable cross-boundary movement. The Yukon River continued as a communication and transportation conduit for Hän (and other Athabascans) and settlers alike, and mobility and contact across the colonial border separating Alaska and Yukon continued unimpeded in the early postcontact period. But a major change occurred at the beginning of the twentieth century with the increased importance of the international boundary between Canada and Alaska. When Alaska was purchased by United States, the boundary had been set to follow the 141st meridian, but it did not significantly affect the lives of Native people at that time. According to Isaac, people had long been moving back and forth across the border and had close ties to each other; Isaac's mother, Louise, was among these (Juneby 2010). This situation is demonstrated by the story of how Isaac's mother ended up at Eagle. Louise Silas was born and raised in Moosehide, in Canada, but at that time the Canadian Hän could come to Alaska and Alaska Hän could go to Canada without concern. Some people who were elderly when Isaac knew them had residences in Canada in the 1930s and 1940s, and many people who are now in Canada had earlier lived in Alaska—they could come and go as they pleased according to the provisions of the 1795 Jay Treaty between the United States and the United Kingdom. Article III states, "It is agreed, that it shall at all times be free to His Majesty's subjects, and to the citizens of the United States, and also to the Indians dwelling on either side of the said boundary line, *freely to pass and re-pass, by land or inland navigation* into the respective territories and countries of the two parties on the continent of America...and freely carry on trade and commerce with each other" (Miller 1931; emphasis added).

Currently, this passage applies principally to Canadian-born indigenous people's access to the United States, while US-born indigenous people have access to Canada based on recognition of (Canadian) constitutional aboriginal rights. The former retains a proof requirement of 50 percent or more blood quantum requirement, and so remains race based, while the latter is predicated on the notion of preexisting aboriginal rights from before Euro-American settlement, and is based on cultural notions and qualifiers (Nickels 2001). As a result of the Jay Treaty, "Native Indians born in Canada are therefore entitled to enter the United States for the purpose of employment, study, retirement, investing, and/ or immigration." Today, this right extends only to indigenous Canadians. Since the passing of the United States' Intelligence Reform and Terrorism Prevention Act of 2004, passports or other qualified documentation are required for border crossing, effectively limiting the freedom of movement provision of the Jay Treaty.

Kinship and relationships continued among the Hän people, of course, whichever side of the border they found themselves on. Isaac's mother, who grew up in Yukon Territory, married Isaac's father, who grew up in Alaska and came to Eagle as part of his job working on the steamboats. If a Canadian woman married an American male, she automatically gained

United States citizenship, and so Isaac's mother came over to Alaska in 1935. Today, everyone crossing the border is required to go through customs, which controls the movement of not only people but also goods, with each country's differing laws having different application to specific items, such as the legality of certain parts of a hunted mammal, feathers from certain birds (i.e., eagle feathers), and the documentation required.

Another consequence of the establishment of the international boundary was changes in trapping laws. Hän people traditionally utilized areas on both sides of the new border, disregarding the imaginary line in the landscape that separated the possessions of the British Empire and the United States. Matthew Malcolm, along with other Eagle Village men, had trapped in the Ogilvie Mountains in Canada. This had been permitted by Malcolm's dual citizenship, but eventually a duty was imposed on furs taken back to Alaska, and so trapping and hunting areas had to be adjusted. In the Eagle area, new territories for trapping and hunting were established from the areas west and north of the village, safely on the Alaska side of the boundary (Caulfield 1979, 12–13; Mishler and Simeone 2004, 56). Such political and management requirements and regulations have steadily increased over the years, significantly affecting indigenous Alaskans' lifeways. Among the latest was the establishment of Yukon–Charley Rivers as a National Monument in 1978 and as a National Preserve in 1980.

Post–World War II Hunting and Other Laws

An important government action that changed Alaska Native societies and cultures was the establishment, after World War II, of game laws that conflicted with indigenous hunting practices (Caulfield 1979, 13). Isaac explains that the people started acquiring more food from stores as hunting became increasingly difficult (Juneby 2010), a sentiment expressed by Elders from across Alaska. As a result, wage labor grew in importance, and commitment to a job restricted a person's subsistence activities by decreasing time available away from wage work. With money, commercial food was increasingly accessible and hunting was no longer a matter of survival (Mishler and Simeone 2004, 57). Nevertheless, hunting continues to be not only a significant way of acquiring food but also an important aspect of identity as an Alaska Native, and people in Eagle continue to hunt even though they often cannot rely on wild meat for their primary sustenance.

Also in the years after World War II, working for the dredging companies on Woodchopper and Coal Creeks provided a source of income for some Hän families; but again, work was seasonal and it was supplemented by trapping and hunting. Isaac Juneby spent some of his early years in the Coal Creek area because his father worked for a local dredge in the summertime, driving points and being a "cat skinner"—operator of Caterpillar equipment—in order to expose the layers of permafrost for thawing (Juneby 2010; Beckstead 2003, 125). In the wintertime, the Juneby family took care of the camp and cut firewood for the steam-powered dredge, and the three families—the Pauls, the Junebys, and the Davids—stayed at the creeks all year long (Paul 1993; Juneby 2010). They all lived on Snare Creek and worked in the area for about six to eight years during the latter part of the 1940s and early 1950s.

During their time at Woodchopper and Coal Creeks, the women took care of the children and occasionally hunted, and men worked long days at the dredge. When Isaac was older, in 1961 and 1962, he also worked on the dredges. His job was to oil the old dredge so that it ran smoothly and costly machine failures were avoided.

Hän Language

Isaac and his family were able to maintain their strong identity as Hän Hwëch'in in spite of working with industrial equipment for gold extraction in part because of their continued use of the Hän language. Isaac's mother and father spoke Hän to him and his siblings as a first language, and when Isaac went to first grade when he was nine years old, he didn't speak English. The family stayed at Snare Creek, and out of Eagle and away from the English language, so the Davids, Pauls, and Junebys retained the Hän language. They returned to Eagle in 1952 and had to speak English only to get by in the community. Isaac realized that it had been the best thing that had happened to them—to be out there, isolated from Eagle, enabling him and his family to retain their Hän language and culture.

Figure 10. "Sunday School at Eagle." A group of Hän children, early twentieth century. (Courtesy of the Archives of the Episcopal Church)

During the oral history interview for this project, Isaac wrote on a piece of paper, "Language is the expression of our culture and our land," stressing that people cannot describe their culture and their land (and their connection to it) if they don't have their language, since the language derives from generations of experience and relationships with the land. Similar concerns are frequently expressed by Alaska Natives throughout the state, and all lament the loss of their indigenous language as a consequence of missionary and government schools.

Schools

In 1905, the Episcopal Church opened a school in Eagle Village that operated until the 1940s, being reopened in 1953 (Mishler and Simeone 2004, 26 and 204). One of the most memorable schoolteachers was Ole Hansen (BIA teacher from 1925 to 1938), who according to Eagle Village Elders Matthew and Martha Malcolm (1991) insisted that the children use only English as their school language. Nevertheless, Ole was well loved by many, Native and non-Native alike. In 1953, the school was opened at Eagle Village, and youth were required to attend. During this time the families started going to the mining claims only for summers (Paul 1993).

Isaac Juneby also remembered the school practices that were meant to assimilate Native children into the non-Native Anglo-American culture, including the exclusive use of English in classrooms, adherence to Christian ideals and expectations, consumption of non-Native foods, and acceptance of the social superiority of non-Natives (exclusively white people), sometimes enforced with some degree of violence (Juneby 2010). Essentially, a foreign worldview was imposed through education—especially through language suppression. Concerning the Hän language, Isaac was a speaker due to his and his family's isolation at Coal Creek, but even he had to speak it every day in order to retain it. Isaac explained:

It's [Hän] not in schools and it's supposed to be taught at home, and if it's not, it's no good. One has to teach kids from early age and then they will catch on fast. Some people didn't spend the time to relearn those things and we are lucky to have some people who speak the language fluently. (Juneby 2010)

Isaac described how the conditions and consequences of culture change and language loss were facilitated by the school system, its requirement that only English be used, and the removal of children from their own parents' cultural teachings, knowledge, and values:

People lost interest in them [older customs] and don't think it's important. Any Native people, and any elder, would tell you that you have to have your culture, your heritage and your language in order to survive. One needs those three and so you have to regain those. When they went to school they had to speak English and not their Native language. If they didn't speak English, they got punished. That's how we lost it. They call it "assimilation into dominant society," the Westernization of indigenous people. We had to go to their school, we had to do everything they did, we had to do just like them or else.

Adeline Juneby-Potts, Isaac's sister, who also grew up at the Coal Creek dredge camp and was one of the children who started attending school in the 1950s, wrote a vivid description about her transition from their home at Coal Creek to life in Eagle: "It was scary just thinking of going into another world. We'd heard stories of Eagle and some of the family we'd never met." To Adeline, Eagle Village was a strange place with new people and different customs, and she wasn't used to being around lots of other children (Juneby-Potts 1993, 19–20). Adeline's positive memories of Ole Hansen show that not all non-Native teachers and schools were abusive, though the process of assimilation effectively remained. Adeline remembers Ole Hansen:

> Ole Hansen was one of the teachers well remembered by my people. She came as a young woman in the 1920s and lived in the middle of the village at the school building in an adjoining apartment type of housing with no modern facilities. There are some good stories told about this marvelous white woman who took to the Indians, treated them with respect and love. (Juneby-Potts 1993, 20)

By this time, school attendance was mandatory for children. Molly Ames (2011) remarked in her oral history interview for this project that, in the late 1940s, a federal marshal came to their house in the lower Charley River area and threatened the family, saying that if they did not send the children to school, the children would be taken away. Such intimidation and threats often caused parents to comply, fearing government abduction of their children. As would be expected, these situations created an enmity and distrust toward schools and government that continues to be expressed today; partly due to this history, dropout rates still are often high in village schools. Particularly in earlier generations (such as Isaac's), many never completed more than a few years of school, though some would persist through high school (almost always in boarding schools), and in recent times these people frequently emerged as Native leaders.

Isaac was one of these leaders who persisted through high school. After completing eighth grade in Eagle, he went to high school at the Bureau of Indian Affairs boarding school of Mount Edgecumbe in Sitka, finishing in four years. In 1988, Isaac completed his bachelor of arts degree in rural development at the University of Alaska Fairbanks, and twenty-three years later he began the process to return to college to work on his master's degree, though circumstances prevented this from happening. In spite of his deep love for and understanding of his Hän culture, Isaac understood the value in obtaining a Western education and a better understanding of wider American society. He was in part motivated to pursue his education to the bachelor's level so that he could more effectively advocate for his people within the power structures of American society, and so he could better bridge the gaps between cultures. In his later life, especially, Isaac excelled at such cross-cultural communication and cooperation, reaching out to agency, military, and university managers, leaders, and researchers. While he attributed much of this success to his education, Isaac also identified his time in the military and with the regional nonprofit Tanana Chiefs Conference as the source of his ability to work cooperatively across cultures.

Isaac Juneby as a Community Leader

In the early 1960s, Isaac served in the US Army and afterward worked for the Tanana Chiefs Conference as a realty officer. Isaac also worked with the Eagle Village Council in two different jobs and served as chief of the traditional council. During the time of his latest interview, in 2010, Isaac was working as the employment coordinator for Eagle Village. As Isaac explained, "I try to understand the lives of different people to try to help them deal with changes successfully."

Isaac also summarized other transformations affecting life in Eagle that he witnessed firsthand:

> The army built the telegraph, and the highway came in the 1950s, and people started coming in. There were different laws and regulations that change lots of people. Government claimed everything and no longer could people do lots of things they were doing earlier, but they needed permits and hunting licenses. Earlier they didn't have to do that and now you have to have hunting licenses, caribou tags and all those things.

Land claims acts and lots of other acts came through and changed people. The Antiquities Act and National Park Service changed things lots. One is under government and regulations when one is on the land. They do both now [subsistence and wage labor]. Lots of people hunt, but not alone.

Government is supposed to protect their subsistence rights, but regulations and arrests are happening. Subsistence should be going on whether the area is a park or not. Earlier, people could go and get what they needed. People moved here to get out of bureaucracies and suddenly it's happening here and they don't like it.

Bureaucratic management of fish and wildlife resources has led to considerable tension between Alaska Native communities and government entities. While they share a common goal—the protection and sustainable management of living resources—the process remains highly disputed. Values and worldviews are not readily compatible between cultures. When this is coupled with the aggressive enforcement actions by regulatory agencies, the disconnect between bureaucratic managers and local leaders increases, and consequently trust decreases or is lost altogether. Even attempts at comanagement have proven to be little more than perfunctory, since Alaska Native leaders possess no regulatory power that can counter state and federal authority. As a result, local management according to local needs and conditions must sometimes be practiced with subterfuge and secrecy, since some regulations effectively criminalize traditional management practices, including the occasional destruction of beaver dams for the well-being of other species such as whitefish and moose. This is often done covertly to avoid potential prosecution.

Isaac explained that in Canada, Native people can hunt whenever they want and are not regulated by anyone other than their own people (this has come through First Nations' land settlements and agreements, and is limited to particular areas delineated within these settlements). People with dual citizenship can hunt in Canada, but those who do not have dual citizenship cannot. People are able to obtain dual citizenship if they can prove that one of their parents is from Canada, but this has proven quite difficult for some.

These days Eagle and Dawson Hän people still maintain relations by inviting each other to potlatches and other celebrations. Eagle continues to hold a potlatch that is similar to those of the past, but they don't have anybody who sings and dances. During those times they invite the Dawson-Moosehide people, but in winter it is sometimes hard to get into Eagle. In summertime, Dawson-Moosehide people sometimes participate in Eagle's events.[3]

Isaac explained that Dawson people have reestablished drumming and dancing as per instructions by Laura Sanford from Tok. They have a band and a singing group, and they practice regularly. Isaac frequently referred or alluded to their revival of drumming, dancing, and singing with pride. Eagle people do not currently have an equivalent group, though Isaac had a drum that he used now and then. The revival of traditional dance included the return of the *gänhäk*—the ceremonial stick the dance leader used to guide his drummers and let them know when to stop or start a song. Isaac explained how the songs and dances are often stories tying people to the land, that this has always been the case, and that this continues since the culture is, in a sense, an "expression of the land" through the people who dwell and depend on that land.

Concerning ties to land, Isaac explained that Elders even say that they belong to the land. One of the great chiefs of the past said, "When I die, I wanna be buried with that dirt." Isaac explained that this means that identity is formed by land, language, heritage, and culture. So the chief meant, "That's part of me, that's how I come, why I want to be buried with it." Isaac thought it made sense. Strong connection with the land, language, and the ability to say, "I know where I come from, I know who my parents, my grandma, my uncles are," will make one a better person, and Isaac lamented the many people who are lost without knowing who their relations are and where they come from.

---

3   Formerly, the Hän could reserve as many seats on the *Yukon Queen II* riverboat as they wanted and received them free of charge. The *Yukon Queen II* ceased operations in 2012, then under the ownership of Holland America Cruise Lines.

Figure 11. Isaac Juneby (July 9, 1941–July 1, 2012) in 2008. (Photo by M. Koskey)

Tragically, Isaac was lost in an automobile accident while visiting his sister in the hospital in Anchorage on July 1, 2012, only a few months before the end of this research. One week later, his sister, Adeline, passed away. Isaac's life is a testament to the survivability and resilience of Hän people in the face of rapid and often severe culture change. As demonstrated through Isaac's life history, the Hän culture of the indigenous people and the Anglo culture of the settlers have blended and been redefined with and by one another for approximately 150 years, though the two remain distinct. Isaac and his family demonstrate the rise of interdependency between the indigenous people and settler people, reflecting a shift in the cultural stories of both peoples and the emergence of a shared history and future. The interdependency was important from the settlers' perspective through the sharing of local, indigenous, traditional knowledge, without which the settlers' lives would have been significantly more difficult in the harsh and unfamiliar Alaska Interior. This is especially well demonstrated in the accounts of the so-called back-to-the-landers, who were mostly young people who came to Eagle in the 1970s to learn indigenous knowledge from the local Hän Athabascans and who would consequently in part carry on old traditions.

ANILCA and Its Effects on Eagle and Nearby Communities

Another force that caused changes to daily life was the creation of the Alaska National Interest Lands Conservation Act (ANILCA), which had profound effects on the communities of Eagle, Circle, and Central through the creation of the Yukon–Charley Rivers National Preserve. In 1978, President Jimmy Carter invoked the Antiquities Act from 1906, which was originally created to protect historic and prehistoric archaeologically important sites from destruction (NPS), to proclaim fifty-six million acres of Alaska as national monuments. The objective was to protect areas that were to become national parks under ANILCA, which was still under discussion at this time (it passed in 1980). The local Yukon–Charley Rivers region that had been proposed to become a national park or preserve was affected by the Antiquities Act, which suddenly and severely limited the activities allowed inside the area.

The application of the Antiquities Act raised objections from many communities throughout Alaska. According to Howe and Brown (1991), who worked for the National Park Service during the initial phases of the establishment of Yukon–Charley Rivers National Preserve, local people felt that setting aside so much land for special public use was unconstitutional. Now the people could not hunt in the area in the same ways as before, for example, which heated emotions in places like Central, Circle, and Eagle, where people openly revolted and demonstrated against the National Park Service, which was governing the withdrawn lands. Bill Brown remembers, for example, when the NPS officials arrived in Eagle one day in 1979 and nearly everyone from the community demonstrated at the airstrip (Howe and Brown 1991).

A more current example of local residents who chafe under government control of the lands they depend on for their subsistence efforts was temporarily resolved by the United States Supreme Court. John Sturgeon from Eagle has been hunting on the Nation River for more than forty-five years. In 2007, twenty years after Sturgeon started utilizing a hovercraft (a ten-foot rubber boat) to access his hunting camp, a new regulation came into effect banning the use of hovercraft. John was stopped on the Nation River and told to remove his hovercraft but was prohibited from even using the craft to return it. This case moved through the court system, taking years of effort and financial investment until John won his case at the Supreme Court. But the Supreme Court remanded the case to the Ninth Circuit Court of Appeals for further review, which then reversed this decision, noting that the law unambiguously supports the National Park Service (Downing 2017). This case highlights a feeling of capricious and seemingly aggressive enforcement of regulations that has little to do with the way in which people carry out their daily and seasonal activities.

Opinions differ, however, and some regional residents perceive the Yukon–Charley Rivers National Preserve as a positive development. Its establishment provided the possibility for studying the entire river drainage of Charley River. Eagle City resident and leader John Borg remarked in his interview (2009) that they probably know more about the country now than ever before. He hopes that this will benefit the state in making decisions about fishing and hunting seasons. John wanted to recognize the National Park Service:

> Prior to the preserve, there were many young couples coming in and establishing themselves at the mouth of various creeks. They were living off the land to the best of their abilities. They tried to make it work. And to make it work was a full-time job between building, gardening, fishing, harvesting moose, trapping for fur. The land claim settlement came in and there were some heavy-handed tactics used to let these people know that they could not trespass on federal land and were asked to leave. A little more compassion should have been given to the people because most of them would have left anyways after accomplishing what they could and that if they were to do anything in their life besides subsisting, they should do it while still capable. (Borg 2009)

In spite of the occasional frustration, this generally supportive perspective was also expressed by Don Woodruff in his interview (2011):

Well, other than the fact that you need to be a lawyer to read the regulations, the state and federal hunting and fishing are becoming more aligned. For example, to hunt caribou, one needs a state and federal permit. Now things are moving towards alignment so that one only needs one state or federal permit to hunt. It's a shame if you need to read the regulations and you can't understand. That is a big issue for lots of people. They don't know what to do when they go hunting, and perhaps they don't go hunting because they want everything to be legal.

Such a personal richness of life in Eagle is demonstrated by the positive outlook of local resident Sonja Sager (2009), who is a descendant of the settlers who came in the 1970s. Most people who lived along the Yukon outside of Eagle fished, hunted, and trapped. When their children were old enough to need standard schooling, many left the subsistence lifestyle behind and moved to a city. Sonja's parents, however, did not move away, and so she got to see other waves of people who were coming to the area to enjoy their retirement years or to raise their grandchildren. Subsistence is also very important for Sonja's family, including her parents and her own children and husband. They grow a garden in early spring and eat from it all summer and harvest things for winter. They also harvest lowbush cranberries from the campground area and blueberries up on the nearby summit. In summer they fish for king salmon, and in the fall they fish for chum salmon for the dogs. Caribou hunting, moose hunting, trapping, and dog mushing are all important (Sager 2009).

Nevertheless, many who came to settle in communities such as Eagle, Central, and Circle did not remain, in spite of the great beauty and bounty of the region. Sonja's husband, Mike McDougal (2009), feels that many people with a similar background to his (coming into the country from out of state) have romantic notions about interior Alaska and about trying to make a living there:

Lots of people come here [Eagle City] and stay for a while but they figure out later that there is limited access to healthcare and to employment and things like that. It takes a certain amount of fortitude to live in a community like this. There is a sense of community and people are helping each other. You need to be a little bit independent too, and to be able to live without many things that people take for granted, like being able to drive to the grocery store. That's what makes people leave.

In spite of often-challenging conditions, both natural and political, the people of Eagle—Natives and settlers alike—continue to practice ancient and shared traditions that enable community resilience and adaptation through interdependency, while maintaining the cultural diversity that has long characterized Alaska.

Eagle and the 2009 Yukon River Flood

Cooperation between community members continues to the present, especially in times of stress or loss, as characterized by the 2009 Yukon River flood that devastated the City of Eagle and, especially, the Village of Eagle. With the move to settled communities in the late nineteenth/early twentieth century, the movements of the subsistence round no longer enabled people to avoid the periodic flood of the Yukon River, and this event took on a more important and disastrous role.

Flooding is a major fact of life in Yukon River settlements such as Circle and Eagle. The intense Arctic cold of the winter is followed each spring by warming that causes the winter snowpack to melt. Some years this is a considerably faster melt than others. Rapid snowmelt causes runoff to flow over the top of frozen ice or ice-jammed channels and can cause widespread flooding. Even with the slowest melts, the ice may jam in areas, acting like a dam that causes the water behind it to flood. Every breakup is different, and some are more harmful than others. The yearly breakup of the Yukon River is accompanied by sounds of ice pushing and shoving against banks, trees, and other pieces of ice, which is greeted with joy for the returning warmth and trepidation due to the possibility of flooding. A post in the Circle campground records some of the high-water marks, revealing the height of the floods. The spring of 1989 was officially declared a flood disaster for Circle. Such floods can be destructive and life-threatening, but the flood of May 2009 that impacted Circle and, especially, Eagle (among other Yukon River communities) was without compare.

Figure 12. Destructive ice overflow at Eagle during the 2009 flood. (Courtesy of National Park Service)

The 2009 flood, caused by a massive ice jam downriver from Eagle Village, has been described as the worst flooding of the Yukon River on record (though the 2013 Yukon River flood of Galena could certainly challenge this claim). In Eagle Village, all the public buildings and cabins were completely destroyed, including the community hall, village public safety office, health clinic, and St. John's Episcopal Church. In the City of Eagle, the buildings along Front Street were badly damaged or destroyed, and vehicles were overturned, moved, damaged, or lost. Ice chunks the size of vehicles and houses were carried downriver by the flood, shearing off any trees in their path. Flood levels eventually far surpassed the previous record of thirty-four feet, reaching fifty-five feet and inundating low-lying sections of both communities.

National Park Service employee and local historian Pat Sanders (2009) watched the flood and videotaped it. On May 3, she watched the ice rise; the ice was approximately 40 percent thicker than it usually is at that time

Figure 13. Trees and two buildings at Eagle Bluff during the 2009. (Courtesy of National Park Service)

of the year. A week before the flood, Eagle residents experienced temperatures ranging from seventy to seventy-five degrees, and at the same time, there was lots of rain in the high country upriver. Eventually, the heat forced the ice to break, then it flooded downriver or, rather, jammed, destroying all the old sections of Eagle Village. Water flooded main streets and low-lying areas, and ice pushed up one hundred yards in many places.

According to the National Park Service, ten homes were destroyed, and many others were damaged or rendered uninhabitable. At least forty-five residents were left homeless and took shelter at the local school. Eagle resident Mark Malcolm explained that his family and five neighbors had lost their homes: "The houses, they are off their foundations. There is water up to the roofs. I don't think anybody has got any flood insurance around here. Nobody thought it would get this bad." There was also flooding downstream in the village of Circle, including reports of twenty inches of water in the community store (Associated Press 2009).

Figure 14. Flooded Falcon Inn at Eagle during the 2009 flood. (Courtesy of National Park Service)

In spite of the destruction caused by this flood, the people of Eagle soon began to rebuild, led by local resident Andy Bassich, who had to be evacuated by a National Park Service helicopter from his cabin nearby as floodwaters rapidly rose. Bassich quickly organized the Eagle Rebuilding Construction Team (ERCT) and the recovery began. Many locals and outside groups stepped up to help in the reconstruction effort, including the National Park Service staff at Yukon–Charley Rivers National Preserve and Christian disaster-relief groups such as Samaritan's Purse, Mennonite Disaster Services, LightShine Ministries, and Disciples of Christ. These groups traveled to Eagle to help build new houses for the displaced residents.

The City of Eagle and Eagle Village worked closely to put together infrastructure to support disaster recovery. The soldiers at Fort Greely sent a forty-foot trailer with furniture, while the Tanana Chiefs Conference, Interior Regional Housing Authority, Brice Inc., and the Northern Alaska

Figure 15. Debris from destruction of Eagle Village by ice in the 2009 flood. (Courtesy of National Park Service)

Disaster Recovery Services organized donations and deliveries. The Raven's Nook mini-department store in Dawson City, Yukon Territory, donated winter parkas that were transported downriver on the *Yukon Queen II* riverboat, and Carlile Transportation Systems arrived in Eagle with a forty-foot trailer filled with materials donated by The Home Depot store in Fairbanks. In addition, many individuals from Alaska and beyond contributed gifts in the form of money, materials, or labor for the recovery effort. In the end, the generosity of outsiders and the diligence of locals resulted in an effective recovery, as expressed by one Eagle resident:

> Our house is going up at an alarming rate. We are so excited. It is so beautiful. We cannot give enough thanks to the folks of MDS [Mennonite Disaster Services], Samaritan's Purse, and Eagle Rebuilding Construction Team along with all the other volunteers who have come in to rebuild our home and community. We would also like to thank

those who have donated to this amazing project by sending supplies or cash donations. You are all beautiful people! (Juneby 2010)

Eagle Village was rebuilt on higher ground in a previously established residential area about three miles upriver from the City of Eagle. The tribe eventually completed the construction of a new village, with much local and outside help, including a new community center—a log structure called the new Charley's Hall, named for Chief Charley. The new village also has a garage, a cache, a guest cabin, a sauna, and a storage building that could readily be converted to a laundry. The tribe used additional funding from the Indian Health Service and money diverted from other buildings eligible for aid from the Federal Emergency Management Agency to build a larger, fully equipped health clinic that could better serve the broader Eagle and Eagle Village area. Called *Bozt'ow Zho*, or Medicine House, the 2,200-square-foot clinic is almost twice the size of the old one and includes a small lobby, an emergency room, an exam room, a dental room, a lab and pharmaceutical supply room, a large office with room enough for two health aides and telemedicine computers, a behavioral health aide office, a bathroom with shower, and a small apartment for visiting medical professionals (Freeman 2011). Recovery efforts proved effective in the end, though as with any such disastrous event, changes in daily life accompanied recovery, necessarily increasing interdependence between community members and between local communities.

Summary

The current state of Alaska Native and settler interdependency is a story of loss and recovery in the sense that the arrival of settlers and the imposition of their lifeways on the Hän led to culture change. This culture change was slight at first, as the settlers trickled in to pursue fur trapping and trade opportunities. Settlers were soon followed by gold seekers and suppliers, which led to the building of trails and the construction of roadhouses between Forty Mile and Belle Isle, later to become the settlement of Eagle. This need to transport goods led to explorations for overland routes from the Yukon to ice-free tidewaters to the south and the establishment of Fort Egbert in Eagle (1899–1900), which itself was designated as the first station of the Washington-Alaska Military Cable and Telegraph System (WAMCATS). The establishment of the Yukon–Charley Rivers National Preserve in 1978 brought many changes that affected indigenous and settler Alaskans alike in both positive and negative ways.

During this period, settlers borrowed and learned much from the Hän and other indigenous peoples of the region, but they also had immediate influence on the Alaska Natives, particularly in terms of material culture. Firearms and manufactured goods were first to be adopted, followed by Western-style clothing and, eventually, more intangible aspects of settler culture, particularly Christianity and the Western/Christian worldview. In reality, this shift in worldview and spirituality was syncretic, resulting in indigenized forms of Western cultural traditions, and following a long line of syncretization common since the spread of Christianity throughout the Mediterranean, Europe, and the wider world. Fundamentally, then, the indigenous worldview persisted and was modified by the settlers' worldview. The opposite also occurred but with much less frequency and intensity due largely to power and population differences.

It can be said, then, that the processes of culture change among the peoples of Alaska's central-eastern Interior were mutually influential, with heavier effects occurring among the settlers earlier and more profound changes affecting the indigenous peoples later. Besides the obvious factor of population differences as more and more settlers arrived during the gold rushes, later government-planned and settler-enacted policies of proselytization and assimilation were instrumental in creating dependency, acculturation,[4] and displacement among indigenous peoples. Despite these processes, Alaska Natives maintain separate cultural identities and customs, though in a way that is today inescapably interdependent.

In current conditions, interdependency partly enables cultural revitalization. Though this may sound contradictory, in fact this is the case due to the increased intercultural tolerance that has emerged in recent decades,

---

4   *Acculturation* is the process by which a culture of a society changes following contact with another society and its culture; the process can be circumstantial or voluntary.

in large part stemming from the interdependence between settlers and indigenous people due to economic needs, cohabitation within the larger Eagle community, and outreach efforts by both groups. A notable example is Isaac Juneby's efforts to bring people together through ceremonies and celebrations, including the "subsistence potlatch" that was held annually until Isaac's death. The contemporary toleration of diversity by government laws, agencies, and employees, and among the population, has allowed for a more public expression of cultural differences. Revitalization is openly practiced, garnering much support from non-Natives, both locally and regionally. This is evidenced by the state's Alaska Native Language Preservation and Advisory Council, whose representatives are speakers and scholars of Alaska Native languages, and which was established by the Alaska Legislature in 2012. Other examples include more frequent and more public Alaska Native cultural events, including potlatches, culture camps, and efforts for the revitalization of Alaska Native languages in public schools and workshops. Now celebrated and vigorously revitalized, identity based on cultural uniqueness is frequently discussed in public forums, as illustrated throughout this text, and by Isaac's efforts throughout his life to maintain his own language and culture.

As a culture bearer for his people and through his work at restoring Hän language use, reviving traditional dancing, and practicing subsistence activities, Isaac demonstrated that there was much to take pride in from one's Native culture. Now that tolerance toward Alaska Native cultures and their diversity has been achieved in Alaska, many from all cultures are better able to understand and even adopt traditions from beyond their own culture. More so than ever, this mutual tolerance is leading to a blending of cultural traits, while at the same time expressions of cultural and ethnic identity are more pronounced. Though seemingly paradoxical, this situation of tolerance nevertheless promotes acculturation while providing social space for identity expression. This culture change also represents an evolution of both indigenous and settler lifeways as acculturation gradually blends some customs and activities.

In this chapter we provided the most in-depth demonstration of the coming together of two peoples from very different backgrounds, and the gradual interdependence that emerged. The settlers, mostly miners but including others from various walks of life, came to realize and respect the knowledge of the Hän and other indigenous peoples already surviving on the lands and waters of the central-eastern Interior. Likewise, the Hän came to adopt many of the lifeways of the settlers—especially in terms of education, technologies, spiritual beliefs, and, later, most aspects of material culture as well.

In the next two chapters, we demonstrate how the interdependency and acculturation that rose from cross-cultural contact varied from place to place as we move to the other side of the Yukon–Charley Rivers National Preserve to the communities of Circle and then Central. Both of these communities are closely linked historically and, as in Eagle, much sharing of traditions occurred. In Central, the settler population is by far in the majority, whereas in relatively nearby Circle (thirty-three road miles northeast), indigenous Gwich'in Athabascans are predominant. Nevertheless, the links between these two communities are many, and both are much more heavily defined by their gold-mining past and present than in Eagle. As with Eagle, local residents will be the focus in order to provide an inside, resident-based perspective on local history and culture.

THREE

A Story of Circle, Alaska

ALASKA'S STEESE HIGHWAY ends on the south (or left) bank of the Yukon River at the town of Circle, or Circle City, variously written in Gwich'in as *Dan Zhit Khaiinlaii* and *Danzhit Hanlaii*. The community's approximately one hundred residents (ACDO, US census population, 2010) are predominantly Gwichyaa Gwich'in, though other Gwich'in from the surrounding region, as well as non-Native families, also live in the community, and the Circle community has a long history of cross-cultural interdependence. In its heyday, Circle City was known as the "Paris of the North" with a population of at least eight hundred miners, traders, transporters, and others, but at times thousands of nonresidents might be present. Then, as today, residents depended on nearby Birch Creek, where gold was discovered in 1892, and on the Yukon River for fishing, hunting, and trapping activities. Placer mining also remains important in the region. Circle is located downriver from Eagle, approximately 150 miles to the northeast, across the area known today as the Yukon–Charley Rivers National Preserve.

Currently, Circle is a predominantly Native community with a Traditional Council (equivalent to an Indian Reorganization Act Council). The village corporation is called the Danzhit Hanlaii Corporation and, as with Eagle Village, regional Alaska Native corporation membership is with Doyon, Ltd., located in Fairbanks. The histories of the communities of Circle and Central are directly linked by their locations, the raw materials found there, and the people who inhabit the area. Families have moved from one community to the other, and people have intermarried, linking family ties closer together. Originally established and settled by non-Native miners and supporting businesses, Circle is today a mostly Alaska Native (Gwich'in) community, and therefore is considered an Alaska Native village. Jobs and other economic opportunities have brought together workers from both Circle and Central.

Circle increasingly came to be a predominantly Gwich'in Athabascan settlement throughout the mid- to late twentieth century, as Alaska Natives remained while many settlers departed with the ever-decreasing employment following the downturn of mining opportunities in the region. This eventually led to an overall decrease in economic activity, and traffic on both the Yukon and overland routes was greatly diminished. The Steese Highway, which opened in 1927–1928, linked Fairbanks through the newly constructed Alaska Railroad to an ice-free saltwater port in Anchorage. This decreased the importance of Circle as the supply point for the Tanana Valley, which led to the gradual disappearance of steamship traffic along the Yukon River. Prior to this, steamers carried supplies from the Bering Sea up the Yukon to settlements along the river. In this way, Circle became the first settlement along the Alaska portion of the Yukon River to gain road access to the outside world (Darbyshire and Associates 1990a). William (Bill) and Vera Strack established a freighting service on the Yukon with their boat, the *Queen Donna*, to provide goods and transport between Yukon River communities and to the Steese Highway's terminus at Circle. Bill took on a deckhand, Albert Carroll, one of James A. Carroll's sons.[1] Albert's life is one of the focuses of this chapter, and his life story is a window into Circle's history. But first we provide an account of Circle's indigenous Gwich'in First People, the settlement's establishment, and its rise, from before Albert Carroll's time.

---

1   James A. Carroll is discussed below under the heading "Albert Carroll's Story and the Community of Circle." An account of his life, derived from his journals, was published as *Above the Arctic Circle: The Journals of James A. Carroll 1911–1922* (2005).

First Encounters and Knowledge of the Gwich'in

The earliest recorded encounter between Gwich'in and Europeans occurred on July 9, 1789, when Alexander Mackenzie and his band of explorers encountered several families fishing just above the delta of what would come to be called the Mackenzie River in Canada. Referred to as the *Loucheux* (indicating "squinters" or "cross-eyed" and rarely used), this term generally refers only to those Gwich'in who dwelled in the vicinity of the lower Mackenzie River and its delta, though it has also been used as a term for the Gwich'in of Canada in general. Later referred to as *Tukudh* by Anglican missionaries, the Gwich'in most commonly refer to themselves as *Dinjii Zhuu*—the "small, or humble, people," though this term applies to all First Nations (Native Americans). The term *Gwich'in* is said to best translate as "one who dwells" or "resident of the region." The indigenous people of Fort Yukon and Circle (and surrounding areas) tend to refer to themselves as *Gwichyaa Gwich'in*, variously said to mean "lowlanders," "dwellers on the flats," or "[Fort Yukon area] dwellers." On the upper Yukon (in Canada), it is said to translate as "giant people" (Slobodin 1981, 532), though the Gwich'in of the Yukon Flats tend to use the term *Nantsaii* to refer to the "giant people" who are said to have crossed from Siberia into Alaska, enslaving the indigenous peoples. This accounts for the origin of another autonym of the Gwich'in—the Ch'itsy'aa, "helpers" or "slaves" (P. Williams, personal communication, 2013).

In the early 1800s, in an effort to initiate trade with the Gwich'in, the North West Company of British Canada established Fort Good Hope (Gwich'in: *Rádeyîlîkóé*; Northwest Territories). However, from the time of its foundation, hostilities between the Gwich'in and Iñupiat (Eskimo of Alaska's North Slope and some neighboring regions) were reported. Fort McPherson (Gwich'in: *Teet'lit Zheh*; Northwest Territories) was subsequently established in 1840 on the nearby Peel River to help avoid this conflict. The establishment of Fort Yukon (Gwich'in: *Gwich'yaa Zhee*) in Alaska in 1847 by Hudson's Bay Company, in what was officially Russian territory, soon followed. The establishment of these trading posts was primarily motivated by the great economic potential of the northwest

Figure 16. "[Athabascan] Indian at Circle City, Alaska, June 1901." (Fred Henton Collection; Anchorage Museum, B1965.018.26)

North American fur trade, soon to be augmented by the western Arctic whaling boom and the Klondike gold rush (Slobodin 1981, 529).

With the rise of trade also came two elements that would forever alter the culture of the Gwich'in: epidemic diseases and Anglican (Episcopal) and Roman Catholic missionaries. From the 1860s to almost 1930, diseases such as scarlet fever and measles, among others, wracked the Gwich'in. With their communities severely depopulated and traumatized, the Gwich'in assimilation into Anglo-American lifeways accelerated. During this time, the influence of the *Dinjii Dazhan*—the "magical people" or medicine men (also referred to by non-Natives as "shamans")—waned as their capacities for healing the unfamiliar diseases proved insufficient. Into this social space came the missionaries, many of whom possessed access to Western medicines to treat these diseases. As would be expected, diseases took the youngest and the elderly in the greatest numbers, and it has been noted that much traditional knowledge passed away with the

Figure 17. "[Athabascan] Indian boys at Circle City, Alaska, catching crackers and cake tossed to them by passengers on steamer J. P. Light." (Fred Henton Collection; Anchorage Museum, B1965.018.46)

untimely death of a community's Elders. Such a loss of the accumulated knowledge of multiple generations inevitably led to rapid culture change.

One example of the severity of culture change through contact with outsiders was revealed in September 1987, when an earthmover crew under contract to build a new Circle airstrip made a startling discovery. The airfield was being moved from the center of the community, where it had been since 1939, to a location beyond the edge of the village. The crew found up to nine graves as they prepared the land for construction. George O'Leary, a long-term resident of the Circle-Central area who had grown up in Circle, investigated the site and discovered a nearby area that contained between ten and twenty additional graves. George spoke to his mother, Elsie O'Leary, who remembered the so-called Spanish flu epidemic that hit Circle City during the spring of 1918. In order to isolate the children from the influenza, Elsie's father, the freighter Nels Rasmussen, had his family (along with several others) taken to a farm a few miles outside of Circle. The Principal Saloon building was turned into a hospital for victims of the flu, and the back room was used as a morgue. Elsie thought that since it was spring and people were worried about flooding and the contamination from flu victims' graves, Nels Rasmussen had allowed a new cemetery to be started at the edge of his homestead, which was located on higher ground. This discovery highlights the dramatic loss of knowledge within the community and the importance of oral tradition.

Foundations of Circle

The founding of Circle in 1893 and nearby Central in 1894 begins with the discovery of gold in 1892 by Sergei Cherosky[2] and Pitka Pavaloff, both mentioned here and in the next chapter due to their importance to Central as well as Circle. Their descendants stayed in the area, hauling freight, delivering fuel, running roadhouses, creating sawmills, and operating gold mines while at times hunting, fishing, and trapping—in short, earning a living. One living descendant, Mary Warren, helped with this document and keeps ties with Circle and Central today. According to local legend, and according to local historian Melody Webb, Cherosky and Pavaloff were hunting and gold panning when they first found colors, or gold, in 1892. In order to spend more time prospecting in the area, they approached Leroy "Jack" McQuesten at his store at Forty Mile for a grubstake—a provision of materials to a prospector for a share of a potential find. The two half-Russian, half-Native men (Creoles[3]) went downriver and collected their families to build a cabin to winter in at a location that became known as Old Portage, which was on the Yukon River fairly close to the present site of Circle City. A hundred other miners with their ears tuned to any rumor of a gold strike somehow heard of the possibility by Birch Creek and showed up to build cabins at Old Portage (Webb 1977,

---

2   Webb spells the name "Sorresca," while other sources use names such as "Cherosky" or "Cheroski."

3   During the Russian period in Alaska, the term *Creole* (креол) designated a person of mixed Russian and Alaska Native ancestry, who was usually an offspring of a Russian male and Alaska Native female.

Figure 18. Miners at "22 Below" gold claim on Deadwood Creek, ca. 1905. (Olson Family Collection, Circle District Historical Society)

90). An entrepreneur would build a store there to accommodate the hopeful miners. In the spring of 1893, Pavaloff and Cherosky crossed the pathless muskeg-and-swamp country to the headwaters of Birch Creek. The other miners trailed closely behind them, fanning out to make gold discoveries on numerous creeks in the area.

Sometime in 1894, Jack McQuesten joined the storeowner from Old Portage in the Circle area. During the flood of spring breakup, some of the cabins near the store were washed away, leading the town site for Circle City to be staked a little farther downriver.[4] The town acquired its name from miners who mistakenly thought they were at the Arctic Circle. (The Arctic Circle, located at 66°33'47" north latitude, is approximately fifty miles north of Circle City.) McQuesten moved to the new town site and offered to grubstake any of the Forty Mile men who wanted to relocate

---

4   The town site was staked by Robert English and Barney Hill on June 24, 1894 (CDHS *Some Dates to Remember*).

Figure 19. "Circle City, Alaska. Taken at midnight on Yukon River, June 21, 1901." (Fred Henton Collection; Anchorage Museum, B1965.018.40)

(Webb 1977, 90). John J. Healy, a representative of the North American Transportation and Trading Company, also had a store at the Forty Mile gold claims in 1892. Following the gold strikes, Healy, like the miners, relocated to Circle in 1894 to offer McQuesten some competition. A settlement of Athabascans (mostly Gwichyaa Gwich'in) grew both within the community and two miles downriver. Freighting services were also established to service the growing number of miners. These two trading posts served approximately three hundred people (Gates 1994, 115).

Within a year the population had more than doubled, and saloons and gambling establishments had been added. Before the Klondike gold rush, Circle was the largest mining community on the Yukon, with a population that scholars such as Melody Webb estimated at seven hundred in 1896 (Webb 1977, 91). It should be noted that Webb provides the lowest population estimate for this period. Others, like Marjorie J. Hay, wrote that Nels Rasmussen, who was living in the area at the time and providing freight services, estimated there were up to 20,000 inhabitants, though it is likely that the majority were not actually resident. It was noted as the largest log cabin "city" in the world (Oakes 1984).

One early resident of Circle City, Nels Rasmussen, developed his business around the turn of the century in order to serve the gold diggings on the tributaries of Birch Creek. In 1901, he married Axinia, the daughter of Erinia and Sergei Cherosky, one of the men who first discovered gold in the area. They raised a large family in Circle City, and around 1909 they built a many-roomed house, known as the Big House, that dominates the downtown of Circle to this day. One of their daughters, Elsie, married Maurice O'Leary, who continued the freighting business. Elsie and Maurice's son George O'Leary hauled fuel from Fairbanks to the gold mines until the 2000s. Axinia and Nels's daughter Mary and her husband, Frank Warren, operated the Yukon Trading Post, a roadhouse, store, post office, restaurant, and gas station in Circle until the 1970s, when they sold out in order to move to Central. There, the Warrens mined for gold until they sold that enterprise and moved to Fairbanks. Although Frank has passed away, Mary still owns property in Central and spends much of her time there. This is one example of a family of mixed Native and non-Native heritage who has spent generations working at both wage labor and subsistence-oriented jobs while maintaining deep ties to the land and its people, even if required to live in urban areas for employment.

Early Growth and Entrepreneurship

Such rapid growth drew the attention of the federal government, and in 1896 McQuesten became the postmaster of the first United States Post Office to be established north of Sitka and Juneau. He was also the banker and the storekeeper of a two-story log building owned by the Alaska Commercial Company, with a fireproof corrugated-iron warehouse to store all the goods. The town was so large and active that besides the Alaska Commercial Company store, Circle also had many other buildings, businesses, and services. Circle City had an opera house, a theater, a hospital, a jewelry store, eight to ten dance halls and saloons, a hotel or two, a couple of trading posts, roadhouses, three restaurants, laundry services, a gambling house, a dentist, a bakery, a barber shop and bath-house, a couple of churches, a library, a school, and a printing press. The *Yukon Press* was established as a local newspaper that still serves as one of the main sources for the region's early history. Photocopies made by the Circle District Historical Society of an article printed in 1899 by the *Yukon Press* named the following officials located at Circle: Capt. W. R. Richardson, Commander of Troops; Dr. D. B. McCann, Register US Land Office; J. E. Crane, US Commissioner; Col. W. Lang, Deputy Customs Collector; F. M. Canton, Deputy U.S. Marshall; F. L. Bates, Postmaster; and fire commissioners: George F. Bemis, W. R. Wheaton, Wm. Moran, and A. B. Clark, Fire Marshall. In addition to these notables were many other residents, the vast majority being concerned with gold mining in the region.

The miners at Circle organized at least two fraternal orders to provide for the welfare of its members, including the Yukon Order of Pioneers and the Miners' Association of Circle City. The Miners' Association pro-vided an early form of government and justice. They would call a meeting and dispense justice on the creeks and at the town site of Circle City. They also "sponsored a large circulating library" (Oakes 1984). As early as 1895, religious services were held in the schoolhouse by Episcopal Reverend R. J. Bowen.[5] He also established a small hospital with two beds.

Besides social services, there were a great many recreational services provided by enterprising entrepreneurs catering to the predominantly male early population of Circle. The saloonkeeper and the dance-hall girls were a vital part of the social life of Circle. One of the best-known gamblers in Circle was known as "Silent Sam" Bonnifield, who did not drink and "was straight as an arrow." He later followed the gold rush to the Klondike and eventually to Fairbanks, where he became a banker (Gates 1994, 124). Another account (Berton 2001) records that Bonnifield died in extreme poverty following a nervous breakdown, reflecting the

---

5   William C. Bompas, leader of the American Missionary Society of the Protestant Episcopal Church, assigned Reverend R. J. Bowen to the new settlement at Circle (Webb 1977, 174).

boom-and-bust conditions that could affect anyone involved in the mining economy, whether miner or businessman.

The entrepreneur George Snow, his partner, Byron Allison, and Snow's family ran a theater they named the Grand Opera House. They performed old-time favorites such as *Uncle Tom's Cabin* to entertain the miners. In March 1896, the Tivoli Theater was constructed. Six women and five men played the same show for seven months, charging $2.50 admission (Gates 1994, 125). The Circle City Miners' Association sponsored a third log opera house. The married women sponsored dances every two weeks, where some of the social divisions within the community came to the fore: Native and white women were welcome, but Native men were not.

Gates also writes of a woman who exemplifies the ideals of entrepreneurism and the changing roles of single women. Mrs. Wills, a widow from Washington, "set up a bakery and sold loaves of bread to the miners at one dollar a loaf, twenty-four loaves per day. She filled in her spare time washing, ironing, and mending, and was in great demand. This hardworking woman was one of the lucky ones; she later left the North with a quarter of a million dollars" (Gates 1994, 118).

Circle City was the main supply point for the mines within the Circle Mining District. The steamers coming through the region from the north and south would stop at Circle City to unload supplies and take on wood for fuel. Trails between the gold diggings on Birch Creek and its tributaries and Circle City were quickly established. Winter became the prime time to travel overland, as the swampy muskeg hardened into serviceable trails. Frozen ground was much easier and faster to traverse by horse-drawn sled or dog teams. Thus, goods would be ordered a year in advance, come up the Yukon River, and be offloaded at Circle to be stored until freeze-up. Then the goods would make their way to the gold-bearing creeks in the Circle Mining district during the winter months.

In 1906 and 1907, a wagon road was constructed from Circle to the mines. At first, the freighter Nels Rasmussen utilized mules to haul freight and follow the trails to the camps along the creeks. Two of the mules, smaller than the rest, were called Kid and Dick. The story goes that if Kid was carrying a case of eggs on his back and the trail led between two trees, he'd move gingerly first to the right, then to the left to get through. Failing this, he'd back up and go around one of the offending trees. Seldom was an egg broken (Hay 1976, B3).

Rasmussen eventually switched to Clydesdale horses, using six horses to a team. At one time he owned sixteen horses (Hay 1976, B3). During the winter, he would also haul ice blocks from the Yukon River for families who used them in their cold storages, keeping foods from spoiling in the summer heat (Babcock n.d.). Rasmussen would stop at the roadhouse at Jumpoff, about twenty-two miles from Circle. There he owned land that he planted with oats and grain to feed the horses throughout the winter. Rasmussen also owned and operated a sawmill—anything to try to earn a living in the country.

Roadhouses

With the trails came roadhouses, established about every twenty miles for the rest and relaxation of the miners and freighters bringing supplies. Some of the early roadhouses were Twelvemile House, Porcupine House, and Ferry, all on Birch Creek; Hogum Roadhouse on Deadwood Creek; Miller House on Eagle Creek; Mammoth House on Mammoth Creek; and Jumpoff and Central House on Crooked Creek. For a complete discussion of roadhouses, see chapter 4 below about the community of Central, which began as Central Roadhouse.

Freighters and Transport

Arthur T. Walden was a freighter who ran a dog team and utilized the trail-and-roadhouse system on both the Yukon and on Birch Creek. In his 1928 book, *A Dog Puncher on the Yukon*, he describes the cold that settled in for weeks during the winter, when it would not get above –60 Fahrenheit. Running his dog team for long hours, Walden was often outdoors, and he commented on the prevalence of frostbite and the freezing of body parts exposed to the frigid air. Mushing his team into and out of the town of Circle during the winter of 1896, Walden notes that the community should have been called the City of Silence due to the extreme cold and lack of outdoor activity:

> People have an idea of a "roaring mining camp" but in this town in the summer nothing but pack trains plodded through the soft muck of the streets; there was no paving; no wagons, no factories, no church bells, not even the laughter of women and children. There was little or no wind in this part of the country. The screech of a steamboat's whistle in the summer, sometimes weeks apart, and the occasional howl of dogs were only part of the great silence. In the winter time the silence was still greater. (Walden 1928, 42)

He goes on to describe the smudge pots smoldering during the summer months in front of everyone's door to keep the mosquitoes away. Gambling was prevalent, and "[o]nly gold dust was used as barter at the stores: this had to be weighed out for every purchase, and it was considered a matter of courtesy to turn your back while a man was weighing it" (Walden 1928, 47).

In January 1897, Walden brought letters down the Yukon from Forty Mile (near Eagle) to various partners in Circle about the finding of gold in the Klondike. Within a few short hours, the price of dogs had skyrocketed, and the price of cabins plummeted as many men began to haul several months' supply of food, their camp outfit, and their mining tools—consisting of pick and shovel, gold pan, and high rubber boots—upriver to the Klondike (Walden 1928, 75–78). Walden was not the only freighter in the area, and others, such as Nels Rasmussen, prospered in this transport and trade business.

It is important to note here that the creation of the Steese Highway represents a significant historic shift in transportation and supply away from the Yukon River inland to the mines. After the completion of the Richardson Highway (in 1898 as a pack trail, and in 1910 as a wagon road) and the Alaska Railroad (1914), the direction of supply was from Fairbanks out to the Yukon. Steamboats continued to provide river access, but the overland trail was year-round. Mary Warren's relatives

Figure 20. Yukon Trading Post, Circle, Alaska. (Frank and Mary Warren Collection, Circle District Historical Society)

Figure 21. Main Street in Circle in 1899. (Pillsbury & Cleveland, photographer, Library of Congress, 2007661331)

were critical to the road freighting and mail delivery overland (see below for a more in-depth discussion of the Steese Highway).

The discovery of gold in the Klondike led to the rapid depopulation of Circle, which was further exacerbated by the discovery of gold near Nome in 1899. Nevertheless, some miners and their families remained, working at nearby Mastodon Creek, Mammoth Creek, Deadwood Creek, and Crooked Creek, and in the upper Birch Creek area in general (ACDO). Though the stampede to the Klondike (Yukon Territory, Canada) emptied some of the country, a few persistent miners hung on and kept the community viable. In the fall of 1898, there were eighty miners left in Circle. The steamers passing Circle during that summer had not left food there but had continued up to Dawson, where their wares could fetch better prices. The miners held a meeting and decided the next boat to pass Circle would be asked to leave eighty outfits of food, and if the captain refused, the miners would force him to do so. The steamer *Portius B. Weare* was stopped and held for three days until the miners boarded the steamer and took eighty outfits from the hold, then paid for them in cash. The storekeeper in turn paid each man for unloading the boat. The boat was then allowed to proceed upriver to Dawson (Walden 1928, 98–102). Riverboats have long been important in Circle for transport of people and goods, and Albert Carroll was one of the most well-known of the Yukon River pilots.

Albert Carroll's Story and the Community of Circle

During August 1910, James A. Carroll of Minnesota landed in Circle aboard the steamer *Sarah*. Following the lure of gold, he hiked to the gold diggings on the creeks flowing into Birch Creek. He worked at various jobs, including as a cook, a handyman, and in the freighting business for Nels Rasmussen. Ultimately, what kept him in the area was not the lure of gold but a love for the land and its people and a way of living. He married a Gwich'in woman from Fort Yukon and founded a family that has spread throughout the Yukon Flats and beyond.

In his published journals, *Above the Arctic Circle: The Journals of James A. Carroll 1911–1922* (2005), Carroll comments on the seasonal rounds of the Native Gwich'in people. During the summer they set up fish wheels. "In those days natives never lived in town during the summer months, they preferred to live in tents up and down the Yukon River or on smaller streams like Birch Creek" (Carroll 2005, 20). After the fish were cut lengthwise and crosswise, they were hung on racks to dry. After fall hunting, the people would return to Circle to spend the winter with a ton or so of dried fish to sell to the traders or mail carriers, who used dried fish for dog food. Carroll's many descendants are still living in Circle and Central (as well as Fort Yukon, Birch Creek village, Chalkyitsik, and Fairbanks). Many continue to fish with homemade fish wheels along the Yukon River during the summer months and hunt during the fall and spring, as well as trap during the winter.

The life of James's son, Albert Carroll, dramatically illustrates the history and current sociological aspects of the people from the village of Circle. Born of a gold-seeker father and an Alaska Native (Gwich'in) mother, Albert met and married Alice Joseph, a Native woman who grew up in a woodcutting camp on the banks of the Yukon River. The wood her family cut powered the sternwheelers that plied the Yukon River. Together Alice and Albert raised a family of ten children on the banks of the Yukon River in Circle. In order to provide for his family, Albert mixed a lifetime of wage labor and subsistence activities, teaching and participating in the old ways while incorporating new ways and changes in technology. This is a trend that continues to the present.

But it was the river—particularly the Yukon—that called to Albert most intensely. Unlike the Mississippi River, the Yukon has no channel markers for boats to follow, and often guides who were familiar with the area would be hired to bring the sternwheelers and other boats safely to harbor. Albert, like many other Native people of the region, possessed the skill to navigate the braided channels of the Yukon River. The Yukon is difficult to navigate since the main channel shifts as the spring breakup of ice tends to change the course of the river, sometimes carving a new path and other times moving into older flows. The main channel meanders within the riverbed itself and has shallow spots and numerous sandbars that are extremely difficult to spot in the muddy water. Albert Carroll was a master at reading the river and displayed an uncanny ability to navigate

Figure 22. Albert Carroll in 1998. (Courtesy of Linda Smith)

its difficulties. His father-in-law, Stanley Joseph, was instrumental in passing on his knowledge of the river and how to read it.

Not having completed many years of formal schooling, Albert was not a good reader or a competent test taker. When he decided to take the coast guard's riverboat pilot exam, he had to figure out another method of proving his competence. He, along with Roy and Sharon Smythe of Fort Yukon, had purchased the *Brainstorm* with the intent of barging materials up and down the Yukon, Porcupine, and Black Rivers. Albert needed his riverboat pilot's license. He passed the exam by drawing the area of the Yukon River on which he wanted to barge goods with all its sloughs and channels. It took him three days to draw a map accurately depicting the Yukon with its major tributaries, islands, channels, and sloughs upriver from Dawson all the way downriver to Beaver, including the Porcupine and Black Rivers that are tributary to the Yukon—a distance of approximately 950 river miles. After offering this map to the coast guard, Albert was very proud to be granted his license. For many years he captained the *Brainstorm*, barging materials up and down the Yukon, Porcupine, and Black Rivers.

Albert also owned a flat-bottomed riverboat with an outboard motor, as do many of the people of Circle. During the summer months, he would establish a fish camp and build a fish wheel to harvest salmon and other fish. Over the years he shared his knowledge of fish-wheel construction with others, including his sons and daughters, many of whom also have riverboats and fish camps with locally built fish wheels to this day. He was always generous with the salmon he caught, and he shared, bartered, and traded his fish with members of the community.

Albert Carroll's Native Heritage: The Denduu and Gwichyaa Gwich'in

Linguistically and culturally related to the Hän Athabascan people of the Eagle-Moosehide-Dawson region are the Gwich'in Athabascan people of the Yukon Flats, the eastern Brooks Range, the Crow Flats, and surrounding areas. Spread over a wide area straddling Alaska, the Yukon, and the Northwest Territories, the Gwich'in are themselves divided into dialect-based ethnic groups that are nevertheless closely related through intermarriage. Of these Gwich'in groups, the Denduu ("Foothill Mountain People") and especially the Gwichyaa ("People of the Flats") traditionally inhabited the lands in and near Circle (Raboff and Kari 2011).

At the time of European contact (middle to late nineteenth century), the Gwich'in Athabascan peoples of the northeastern interior of Alaska and the northern and northwestern reaches of the Yukon and Northwest Territories were divided into either nine or ten regional bands (Slobodin 1981, 515). Each of these bands continued to use their dialect of the Gwich'in language through the time of their transition from seasonal nomadism to the establishment of permanent communities in the twentieth century. For example, it was the establishment of the trading post that tied the people to the specific location of Circle City. This summary focuses on the Denduu and Gwichyaa Gwich'in.

Though the subsistence economy was based on the hunting of large mammals—particularly caribou—it seems that the bulk of the diet consisted of fish and, to a lesser degree, small mammals. Both anadromous and freshwater fish were widely utilized in the Gwich'in region throughout the year. In the twenty-first century (and in preceding decades) a subsistence-cash economy has arisen with the increase in trade and local demand for trade products. Many of these trade goods are acquired to aid in the practice of the subsistence economy, such as firearms, boats and motors, snowmobiles, and all-terrain vehicles, augmented by perishables such as manufactured food products, fuel, and ammunition. Nevertheless, the subsistence round continues to be followed within all regional communities with a focus on fishing for salmon and hunting moose and caribou, alongside trapping.

Albert Carroll utilized all these technological changes. Besides the frequent use of his motorboat, he also would purchase a new snowmachine almost every fall to aid in his winter trapping efforts. He continued to hunt moose as he was trapping and brought home many animals to share within the community, supplying those who were not as mobile or as lucky as hunters. Furthermore, the snowmachine provided the opportunity for him to make more frequent visits to his family, who stayed in Circle during the trapping season. During the winter, he trapped on the headwaters of the Black River, where his cabin was more than sixty-five miles from Circle on the other side of the Yukon River. Without the use of his snowmachine, Albert would have practiced the routine of his father, who had to leave Fort Yukon during August in order to reach the trap line by boat with his dog team; such a distance and travel by dog team precluded winter visits home.

Evidence suggests that in precontact times Gwich'in peoples were heavily involved in trading (and, to a lesser extent, warfare) with their neighbors, even acting as middlemen in regional trade, especially between those dwelling east of the Mackenzie River and other Athabascan and Iñupiaq-speaking peoples. Albert indicated that his mother's family was one of the established Native trading partners. They guarded their exclusive rights and would travel widely in pursuit of their trade interests.

The importance of trade and wealth in Gwich'in society are well attested, and though no formal socioeconomic ranking structures were used, wealth ranking did occur. In general, wealthy households were accorded greater prestige, and their success was attributed to the capacities of the households' members—a trend still present today (Slobodin

1981, 524). Conversely, poor households were thought to be suffering not because of the faults of their members but as a result of the faults of the community as a whole (Slobodin 1981). The more fortunate shared food with the less fortunate—an inherent expectation in Gwich'in culture.

Throughout the course of the interviews for this project (and in many other personal communications), economic success was described as being a combination of discipline (enabling skill) and luck (reflecting reverence and respect for others—including nonhuman entities such as animals). Thus the individual who possesses little and is suffering is the responsibility of the community, and deprivation is seen as a communal shortcoming. This is further reflected in the deep and widespread ethics of sharing and reciprocity that continue to serve as a symbol of identity among the Gwichyaa and Denduu. As a contemporary example, in fall 2015 the husband of one of Albert Carroll's daughters said he had given up hunting moose, as his freezer was always empty: his wife had a habit of giving all the meat away.

The Gwich'in into the Modern Era

In spite of these deprivations and rapid culture change, the Gwich'in remain a cohesive people who continue to mix ancient traditions with modern practices. This is clearly evident in the acquisition of wild resources, where knowledge of natural indicators, traditional fishing and hunting locations, and the use of modern equipment with traditional methods continue. So, too, continues the use of fish camps to situate oneself to the seasonal movement of fish.

Three issues dominate the contemporary sociopolitical situation of the Gwich'in of the southern and eastern Yukon Flats: ongoing mining in the White Mountains, the possible reintroduction of the wood bison (*Bison bison athabascae*), and the development of natural gas resources. These three issues are intertwined to some degree, primarily due to the status of the wood bison as an endangered species. Due to provisions of the Endangered Species Act, the reintroduction of wood bison could affect the regulatory regime concerning gas and mining development, and some Gwich'in see such development as the key to increasing economic and political autonomy. These positions are not mutually exclusive, however, and the main point of contention seems to be where to place value: on the prevention of economic development to ensure the health of the land and waters, or on the promotion of development to meet very present economic needs? There remains no consensus on these issues at the local level.

The current economy of the village of Circle is based on a mix of wage labor, dividend payments from corporations, and subsistence hunting, fishing, and trapping, as is the case in many other rural Alaska villages. There are a few jobs offered by the school, the clinic, the village corporation, the postal service, and the power company. The one remaining store, the HC Company, offers gas, telephone service, liquor, and groceries to the community. Residents leave the community seasonally for jobs in the Central gold-mining industry, in the petroleum industry on Alaska's North Slope, forest firefighting, and work within the community on anything available. But local cash employment is limited and largely supplements the subsistence economy. The population tends to increase during the summer as jobs become available for construction projects, tourist-related industries, and the subsistence fishing season.

The Gwich'in of Circle still follow a seasonal round of activities. Spring activities include waterfowl hunting as the flocks of geese and ducks come back to the Yukon Flats, as well as beaver and muskrat hunting and trapping. Summer is a time of wage earning, and July is also a time for fishing and drying fish. Fish wheels and nets are primarily used to harvest salmon. Several families still have fish camps along the river that are set up to be lived in during the heavy runs of salmon. Albert had a fish wheel in a camp for many years, and his sons construct and operate the same design to this day. Residents also gather berries such as blueberries, lowbush and highbush cranberries, and raspberries, as well as birch bark for making and selling handicrafts (Darbyshire and Associates 1990b).

Hunting begins in the spring with the migration of ducks and other waterfowl, and it continues during the summer months for bear and during the fall for moose, primarily along the Yukon River and Birch Creek. Caribou are also hunted during the fall and winter when they are available.

Albert was an expert woodsman who hunted throughout the seasons. He organized drives for moose such as those described by the anthropologist Richard Nelson (1986, 107–108). On an island in the Yukon River, Albert would position friends and relatives either on foot, in a boat, or, during the winter, on snowmachines at likely points around the island. Then one or two men would move down the length of the island, driving the moose to the waiting hunters. As is typical of the people of the area, Albert would share his catch of meat with the members of his family who had their own households and others less fortunate or not as successful with the hunt.

Winter is the time of woodcutting for firewood and construction projects and, most important, trapping. Trapping has continued to provide income for some residents in the village. Some families use the fur to create and sell handicrafts, further augmenting the cash economy. Albert was one of the most successful trappers in the village of Circle. He trapped lynx, marten, wolverine, fox, wolves, and mink. He was a master at making snares and routinely set out hundreds during a single season. Typically he would take on a partner for one to three seasons, and in this manner he trained many of the younger generations in the skills and art of trapping, snaring, skinning, and drying the animal hides. He built cabins along the lines he ran, and he used the trapping trails his father had run before him, and blazed new ones as well. He built trap lines on the Black River, Birch Creek, and in his later years along the Yukon.

As an example, during the 1970s and 1980s Albert was trapping on the upper parts of the Black River, about sixty-five or seventy miles cross-country from Circle. His father had trapped in this area since the 1920s. Albert had many partners there, including Owen Stockbridge, a young settler from the community of Central. He trained this young man in the art of snaring and trapping animals, helping him to become, as Owen termed it, a "master trapper," strengthening his bond to the land itself. They constructed a main cabin and set up tent camps along more than a hundred miles of trails with lines stretching out in different directions. Even when they were no longer trapping partners, they remained close friends and would often visit each other, furthering the ties of the two families and, by extension, their communities. This also exhibits a cultural tie between local Gwich'in and settlers.

In the early 1980s, Albert transferred "ownership" of this established trap line to a young couple from Central named Richard and Laurel Tyrrell; Laurel is one of this book's authors, and her family is one of those featured in chapter 4. The transfer of operating trap lines to new owners is a difficult concept. The Native people did not consider ownership of the land, but Albert again adapted to the changing times by "selling" this line. As regulations and land designations began to change, so did the establishment of a trap line. More and more equipment and effort were put into cutting trails and building cabins, which may or may not have had construction permits from the designated landowner. Thus, the transfer of ownership was more of a statement that the previous person would not trap there any longer and the new person would be allowed to have all the equipment and buildings on the trap line located in that designated area.

Traveling in the winter requires a whole different set of techniques than in the summer. The snowmachine (also known as snowmobile or sno-go) has become the major form of winter transportation. Richard Nelson (1986) describes the rigors of winter movement through the Alaska Interior: "The traveler must also know how to find his way unerringly, cope with a wide variety of snow and ice conditions, and be able to predict the weather and adjust to its changes" (170). Accidents or difficulties can literally be a matter of life and death. Albert had many years of experience on the land and accumulated knowledge of the land, the river, and travel through it. His way of living clearly demonstrates the connection of people to the land. Many times during his life he dealt with overflow (water flowing on top of river ice), thin ice, deep snow, bone-chilling cold, and open leads in the river, though he had many techniques for dealing with adversity and dangers.

One way Albert kept himself warm over the years was to hop off his sno-go and start running. He would run until his toes warmed up, then hop back on his machine and continue down the trail. During the 2017 school spring break, Albert passed his knowledge to the younger generations. On Birch Creek at the Tyrrell trap line cabin, three generations gathered to participate in beaver trapping. Three youngsters from six to ten years old arrived whose ancestors, while not Gwich'in, came from Bettles, Emmonak, and Iliamna. All week it was between –30 and –35 degrees Fahrenheit each night, but during the day the sun warmed the land to about –5. The ten-year-old mentioned one day that her feet were getting cold. Immediately her grandmother hopped off her snowmachine and, with the young one in tow, ran, jumped, and stomped down the trail while singing about the "Albert Carroll wiggle." Before long the entire crew of eight or nine people were stomping and romping and wiggling down the trail and singing about Albert Carroll and his cold toes. It took only a short amount of time for everyone to become warm. All ages benefited from Albert's knowledge and expertise, but the youngest ones especially learned an important lesson; they had to repeat the exercise a couple more times before riding the four to six miles to arrive at the warm cabin.

Albert Carroll is certainly the epitome of Richard Nelson's description of the Athabascan man: "Exploiting the boreal forest environment requires a thorough knowledge of the landscape. The Indian must know the precise details of local geography, the favored habitat of each species of useful plant and animal, and all physical features important for travel and safety, knowledge which it takes many years to acquire" (Nelson 1986, 278).

After "selling" his line on the Black River to the Tyrrells, Albert moved his trapping activities closer to home at what he called "Twelvemile," a bluff approximately twelve miles downriver from Circle. There he built a cabin on his Native allotment and lived portions of the year, continuing his hunting, fishing, and trapping activities. His stories of this place incorporated his belief that the "Little People" had a home close by within the bluff itself. He often described seeing these Little People, a term widely used in Alaska (and in many other lands worldwide—i.e., dwarves, leprechauns). One time when he was returning to his cabin, he overturned his snowmachine. He repeatedly tried to push it upright, but it was firmly wedged between tussocks—tight tufts or hillocks of grass that tend to be surrounded by marshy ground. These tussocks, which can grow to three or four feet high, often have deep ditches between them filled with water that freezes during the winter. Again and again, Albert pushed, shoved, and wrestled with the machine. Becoming exhausted, he fell asleep and woke up snug in his bed at the cabin with no memory of arriving there. He claimed the Little People must have offered him a helping hand, as he had been incapable of accomplishing the task alone.

Throughout these activities Albert displayed a skill for meshing modern technology and more traditional knowledge and ways of thinking. A talented barge operator, he still held on to traditional beliefs and practices. One of his early trapping partners, settler Gordon Bertoson of Washington, had lived much of his life at Jumpoff by the confluence of Crooked Creek and Birch Creek. Gordon fished for food for the dogs he boarded during the summer and trapped in various places during the winter. One year, he and Albert built a cabin on Birch Creek about thirty miles below the current bridge in order to trap there for a winter or two. After a long time of working on their lines, Gordon decided it was time for Albert to go home and be with his wife and growing family. Albert was reluctant to leave his partner to do all the work. Gordon decided to play on Albert's belief in the "bushman," known in Gwich'in as *na'en* or *na'in*. According to Albert, his mother, a medicine woman, had once been kidnapped for a time by a bushman, and he was a firm believer in its existence. Gordon strapped something to his snowshoes that resembled a very large foot, then stomped all around the cabin. Albert went home the very next morning.

This story also dramatically illustrates the necessity of leaving one's family for perhaps months at a time while pursuing trapping activities. Alice Carroll stayed in Circle so the children could attend school, and Albert was away from home for long periods. Albert cared deeply about the need not only for his children to have an education but for education in general. The established schools in Circle sometimes mixed Alaska Native and settler populations and sometimes separated them—typical through the 1970s, as well as acting as an agent of change to the Gwich'in way of life.

A story told by Albert's partner, Gordon, further accentuates the changes that occurred in how people went about their subsistence activities. During an oral history interview with Laurel Tyrrell, Gordon told how he came across signs of marten and built a cabin there to trap for the winter. He came across signs of lynx and built a cabin there to trap for lynx in that place for the winter. Over and over, he told of coming across a sign as he hunted or prospected or fished. Laurel finally asked him how many cabins he thought he had built during his lifetime. After a moment of silence, he said, "Thirty or so…"

With the change in land designations due to the Alaska National Interest Lands Conservation Act of 1980, such a way of living is no longer possible. As a result, the traditional knowledge necessary for such activities and lifeways is less frequently passed on to the next generation, thus not only changing the nature of the knowledge but replacing it with learning techniques focused on formal, government-required schooling. This diversion of education from local, place-based, practical skills to universalist, nationalist-oriented, government-sanctioned academic skills can be problematic, leading to stressful culture change.

Education and the School

Formal education in Circle began when pioneer teacher Anna Fulcomer was sent to Circle after a town meeting held in January of 1896, resulting in a petition being sent to the Department of Education (Gates 1994, 120–121). The people of Circle were to provide the schoolhouse and furniture while the Bureau of Education in Washington provided the teacher and her salary, lamp oil, and wood as heating fuel. When Fulcomer arrived, the school was not completed. She began classes with thirty to thirty-six students amidst the construction. There was a mixture of people, including both settlers and Alaska Natives of various backgrounds, from ages five to thirty (Gates 1994, 122).

Nels Rasmussen donated a building to the Territorial School in Circle. He had been operating a saloon in the building since 1910, but when local alcohol prohibition came along in 1918 (national prohibition came into law in 1920), he gave it to the territory to use as a school. It was moved to higher ground, ideally out of the spring flooding zone, where it became a school. Sometime between 1918 and 1919, the Native School burned to the ground and all students then attended the Territorial School in the old saloon. During this time, official policy dictated the separation of Alaska Natives from non-Natives for schooling, so this mixed situation was atypical and temporary.

As was noted in the chapter on Eagle, there were years when the prevailing philosophy of education was to assimilate Alaska Native children into the settler population. In order to accomplish this task, English was the only language allowed while attending school. Larry Nathaniel, a long-term resident of Circle whose family was from Chalkyitsik on the Black River to the northeast, spoke of his experiences while attending a school where he was forbidden to speak his native tongue. Feeling sorry for the younger children, who could not comprehend what the teacher was asking them to do, he would translate for them even though he knew he would be punished for this act of kindness.

In more recent times, in accordance with the Regional Educational Attendance Area (REAA), which had jurisdiction over the school system of Circle and Central, the local people served by the schools could be elected to the board and make decisions on how education was to be carried out. Albert served on the Yukon Flats School District Board of Education. With the advent of this local control, Albert could help to facilitate the emergence of the bilingual program that would teach the young people not only their native language but their customs and traditions as well, within the school's educational programs.

Albert also valued people who had a formal Western education and was outspoken about his own lack thereof. During the summer of 1979, he was piloting the *Brainstorm* up and down the Yukon River and hired a cook to supply meals for him and his two deckhands. The young tourist to whom he offered the job had just arrived in the area. During a conversation one evening while tied up to the banks of the Yukon River, he discovered that this young woman, Laurel Tyrrell, held a teaching certificate. Appalled that Laurel was working as a cook and not utilizing her education, he strongly encouraged her to apply for a teaching position in the Yukon Flats School District as soon as the *Brainstorm* reached Fort Yukon and the regional office. Thus began Laurel's teaching career in the Yukon Flats. Until she was able to establish her own household, Albert shared the contents of his freezer to ensure she had enough salmon, moose, and berries to last the winter.

Currently, Circle is governed by a Traditional Council and elects its leaders. Albert Carroll served as Village Chief multiple times and was a leader within the community in many other ways. His son Albert Carroll, Jr., has also served multiple times as the Village Chief, following the example set by his father and grandfathers before him. Albert passed away on January 15, 2006, leaving his wife, Alice, many children and grandchildren, and a group of friends who had worked with him in multiple capacities to carry on his legacy.

Albert was the epitome of the blending of traditions in Alaska, living practically, self-sufficiently, and cooperatively with others in Circle and beyond. Throughout his life, he practiced his skills in trapping, hunting, fishing, and many other subsistence activities alongside his skills of river navigation, machinery, and building. Widely respected for these skills and the genuine nature of his personality, Albert was also known for his trustworthiness and generosity, and his willingness to pass his knowledge on to others.

The Steese Highway: The Road to Fairbanks

Critically important to the development of Circle City, and crucial to its survival over the years since its foundation in 1893, is the Steese Highway. When gold was discovered in the Tanana Valley in 1902–1903, freight and travelers had to make their way along the Yukon, overland from Circle, and then over the mountains. Though the Valdez Trail was in use by 1903, and the Alaska Railroad by 1925, Circle City was still the place one went to register gold claims, even those located in the Tanana Valley to the south, over the White Mountains. By 1928, the wagon road to Circle and Central was upgraded to a road called the Steese Highway. Since it has remained unpaved from Circle to about the eighty-mile mark, where the pavement begins, many people are currently unaware that the terminus on the Yukon had originally been the starting point of the highway, not the ending point.

Following most of the Circle–Fairbanks Trail that had been developed to reach the mining camps located in the Tanana Valley from the Yukon River, the 161-mile Steese Highway was built in the late 1920s. Completed in 1928, the road was named after General James G. Steese, who, as the president of the Alaska Road Commission, helped to construct the highway. Running from downtown Fairbanks, it ends at the Yukon River in Circle City. It is a continuing economic and transportation lifeline for residents along its route, particularly in the communities of Chatanika, Central, and Circle.

Before the highway was completed, there were a variety of methods of travel. Steamboats plied the Yukon, dog mushers opened trails, people walked, and horses used well-established trails. In 1896, prospectors, miners, their wives and families, and those who provided food and equipment to the people in the area used two main river routes. One route was mostly traveled in winter up the Yukon, down over the mountains to the Gulf of Alaska coast to Juneau (in part the famous Chilkoot Trail of Klondike fame), and then to Seattle. The other route, traveled only in summer, was down the Yukon by steamer to St. Michael's near the mouth of the river, then via a coastal steamer around the Aleutians to Seattle. Three steamers plied the Yukon at this time, all burning wood that was cut near the river, "and the upstream trip of over fifteen hundred miles was so slow that they could not make more than two trips each year" (Walden 1928, 28).

From the Yukon to the gold mines, horses were used, particularly during the winter, to haul freight. "They were plagued by mosquitoes and suffered from the cold" (Gates 1994, 101). Dogs fared better. Six or seven large, heavy dogs were harnessed single file to a freight sled, hooked in three rows (Gates 1994, 103). Trappers usually used a basket-type sled, though most important was a capable lead dog. "A well trained lead dog is the most important member of the team" (Tremblay 1983, 69). Tremblay trapped with dogs into the 1950s. He hitched his dogs in pairs; the two behind the leader are known as "swing dogs," as they swing the team in the direction the musher desires to turn. The next pair is called "team dogs," and the two closest to the sled are known as "wheel dogs." Their job is to break the sled loose and start the sled moving, and these are usually the largest, strongest dogs.

The advent of automobiles brought more summer traffic and even tourists. In 1931, only a few short years after the highway's completion, Norma J. Hog wrote a letter to her mother about her trip over the Steese Highway. She talks about the road commission camps as well.

We took our lunch into a Road Commission mess House at noon as 'twas raining so we thought 'twould be nice to get in. They set tin plates and cups out for us—gave us coffee, tea, pie and cake. I've been in 4 Road Camps now and talk about the big eats! Frosted cakes, jelly rolls, dark and light bread, rolls and rustic meats, salads and pies—why all the things on the table was enough for a king. ... [T]hey are all men cooks in these Road Camps. Our road all the way back to Fairbanks was rutty and muddy as it had rained for hours. Mr. Moore drove very slowly and we had the road almost all to ourselves so we felt safe. (Hog 1931)

Since the winter of 1984–1985 (Bishop 1986), the Steese Highway has remained open year-round, but travel is not always possible. In the winter, blowing snow can cause drifts to block the road even right behind a snowplow, but particularly when the Department of Transportation drivers are not on the job. It also causes a dangerous condition known as a whiteout. The absence of trees on both the Eagle and the Twelvemile summits leads to this dangerous condition where the sky, the earth, the road, and everything else are white. It is exceedingly difficult to tell where the road ends and the sky begins. "It's like being inside a ping-pong ball," says Richard Tyrrell, who recently retired from the Alaska Department of Transportation, where he worked as a snowplow driver on the Steese Highway for thirty years. In 1990, the state installed gates on the summits, so the road can be closed to traffic when the weather becomes too dangerous.

Rick Tyrrell (2010) reports that when the road was opened, it led to changes because the people who came in wanted to develop the area. Many were entrepreneurs who saw Central as a way to make money. They campaigned for the school and similar community infrastructure such as a fire hall and community center. It mystified him that people would relocate to a place where things were simpler but then try to make it like where they came from. The people who had lived in the community before the road opened generally preferred the community as it had been, and did not welcome the changes. During the 1970s and 1980s, a sign was posted at the entrance to the community on the Steese Highway that reflected this sentiment: CENTRAL POPULATION: ENOUGH. The highway also enabled access to others who may not otherwise have come into the community, and Tyrrell (2010) relates a couple of peculiar incidents:

> One guy came in thinking to get seals in the spring. He was going to put sharp stakes in the river so that the seals would be staked when they swam up the river. (No seals are found in the area and that would not reflect a method of harvest either.) Another guy was going to heat his house with chicken manure. His house was only half-finished by August. There's been tons of people like that. They come and try to live off the land, leaving pretty soon.

Travel over the Steese Highway has often connected visitors and residents of Circle and Central alike. It is a long, dusty road with amenities and services available only infrequently. During the summer months, the coarse gravel causes many flat tires. In fall and spring, and during occasional winter thaws, icy patches and slippery road conditions arise that may force a traveler into the ditch. Winter storms create whiteout conditions, as well as bitter cold and drifting snow that can cause frequent road blockages. Caribou and moose on the roadway also create hazardous conditions. Once in trouble, a traveler may wait hours or even overnight for another vehicle to come by or for help of any kind to arrive. On the Steese Highway it is rare for a vehicle to pass by someone in need without stopping to offer assistance. If the driver is unable to pull the vehicle out of the ditch or change a flat tire, a ride is provided to the closest place aid is available. Rick Tyrrell, as a Department of Transportation employee, lost track of how many people he has pulled out of snowbanks or provided some form of aid, while on duty or not. One tourist he tried to help while off-duty was on the side of the road in a pair of shorts during an insufferable mosquito season. He had hit the end of the pavement and the beginning of the gravel surface and lost control of his little rental car. He ended up upside down, fortunately in a dry ditch. When asked if he would like a ride somewhere, such as to the closest phone booth, the man declined, preferring to wait for the state troopers. Rick used his satellite phone to call the state troopers, then handed the phone to the tourist. By the end of the conversation the man realized no troopers were coming, and he called a tow truck.

Most residents of Central and Circle have been in the ditch or had a flat or other mechanical trouble and shared similar experiences of adversity on the Steese. Through the offer of aid to another, and receiving aid themselves, community members have often averted outright disaster. It is a thread of common experience that binds the community together. This story also highlights a difference between outsiders and insiders in the region, as an insider would never leave anyone who is in need, known or unknown, to face the wilderness alone.

Summary

Through the eyes of local individuals and families, some contemporary and others historical, this ethnohistory of the central-eastern Interior of Alaska demonstrates the culture changes that accompanied the arrival of settlers. In Circle, established by settlers for the purpose of supporting the gold rush and associated activities, the coming together of cultures can be seen most explicitly. The customs and traditions of two peoples came to most heavily influence each other, and the outcomes of their interactions across the six generations of over 120 years is evident in day-to-day life. Nevertheless, both Gwich'in and settlers maintain their distinct identities, though much cultural integration and intermarriage has occurred.

Both cultures have changed from earlier forms, and old customs are often set aside as new ones are developed or adopted. The value of not setting aside old customs permanently—in essence, not losing them—has always been a value of the ancient Alaska cultures in particular, and to all cultures in general. While this causes some struggles with issues of identity and self-determination—sometimes complicated by ethnically mixed parentage—for the most part a syncretic cultural blend emerges that ties to both parents' heritages. The valuing of older, seemingly outdated, though not truly anachronistic customs, enables the continued consideration and understanding of the ancient wisdom embedded in these customs. Continuance in the practice of ancient customs is a common value shared by most rural residents in Alaska, whether Alaska Native or non-Native.

The life of Albert Carroll—himself of mixed cultural origins— demonstrates how interdependency came to characterize both identities. Today, the lifeways of Alaska Natives and settlers are sometimes quite similar cross-culturally, and this often extends even to beliefs. While tensions have occurred between these groups, these are the exception rather than the rule, and cooperation remains common and even expected—in fact, it is a skill of survival. Circle and its historical sister settlement of Central are inextricably linked through a shared history and, in many cases, through shared family and friends. Both settlements are living examples of how cooperation, mutual respect, and cultural flexibility maintain community.

FOUR

A Story of Central, Alaska

CENTRAL IS A small community of central-eastern Interior Alaska with a population that fluctuates between 100 and 150 (ADCCED, US census population, 2010). Its residents are involved in mining, service-oriented jobs, trapping, fishing, and hunting. Central, unlike Eagle, was not an Alaska Native community before the arrival of settlers, and today most of its indigenous residents (approximately ten people) are Gwichyaa Gwich'in from the nearby community of Circle, which shares ties with Central through economy, marriages, and the road link of the Steese Highway.

The recorded history of Central begins with its settlement by non-Natives. Nevertheless, the Gwichyaa Gwich'in, and to a lesser extent the Denduu Gwich'in, long made use of and tended the areas surrounding today's community of Central. After the discovery of gold in Birch Creek and its tributaries in the early 1890s, a roadhouse was needed between Circle and the mining operations on Birch, Mammoth, Mastodon, and Preacher Creeks. This roadhouse—Central House—was built around 1894 at the supply trail's crossing of Crooked Creek.

The nearby settlement known as Circle Hot Springs is located eight miles to the southwest of Central on a spur road and is the location of the now-closed Arctic Circle Hot Springs Resort. But it was gold that lured prospectors to the region, and Central continues to be supported by a local economy of trade, bartering, and sharing that crosses cultures and distances between settlements. As the mining economy expanded and contracted, Alaska Natives maintained their uniqueness and separate identities from contact to the present.

Similar values have enabled meaningful cross-cultural communication between Alaska Natives and settlers, creating a blending of customs and recognition of commonality in values. A cultural blending, though limited to some degree by ancestral customs and worldviews, can be seen in the cooperative and collectivist behaviors of Central residents, with clear and conspicuously expressed family-oriented social values and behaviors, including sharing and reciprocity, placing community well-being before personal desires or needs, and community-wide shared decision-making. Interdependency is thereby derived from shared involvement in economic, political, and personal contacts and cooperation, leading to further exchanges of ideas and values. The history of Central is a reflection of these shared values in many ways. As with each rural Alaska community, Central possesses a unique story that is tied not just to the surrounding lands but also to the heritage of its residents' ancestors. The community of Central demonstrates well how the land shapes the people it sustains, regardless of their cultural origins. Its residents hail from a wide variety of backgrounds and places, though a local identity has emerged and serves to bind residents together. As a small, tight-knit community, Central possesses its own unique story of interdependency.

The ethnohistory of Central is drawn from many sources, including local residents and archives at the Circle Mining District Museum, located in Central. This material was collected and written primarily by Laurel Tyrrell, introduced earlier due to her arrival in Circle when she first came to Alaska, and due to the role of her husband, Rick Tyrrell, regarding the Steese Highway, discussed previously. This is yet another example that demonstrates the many connections between the communities of Circle and Central. Laurel, a longtime resident of Central, is a teacher, historian, and trapper. With her husband and children, Laurel has spent her life in a small community in what most would consider a vast wilderness, developing skills and relationships that ensure survival and a thriving family and household. The local and traditional knowledge used by Laurel and her family is similar in many ways to the indigenous traditional knowledge of the Hän and Gwichyaa peoples of the central-eastern Interior of Alaska, and this chapter provides a firsthand insight of changing cultures and conditions in this region. Focusing on the settlers who are the community of Central, and due to Laurel's access and reputation, a great deal of depth and specificity of local culture and history is available.

The focus on the Tyrrell family—particularly on Laurel herself—is presented alongside the history of the Larsen/Olson family. Arriving in the late nineteenth century, the Larsen/Olson mining family remained in the country for generations rather than departing once gold was discovered or resources to search for gold were exhausted. Throughout this ethnohistory of Central, it is evident that the stories of the Larsens/Olsons are largely the story of the community as a whole. As with the Tyrrells, their descendants continue to shape the daily life and culture of the region. But first, we provide a general background recounting the arrival of prospectors and settlers into the Central and upper Birch Creek mining areas.

The Arrival of Settlers and the Discovery of Gold

Historical records show that one event heralds the great transformation that affected indigenous Alaska societies: the arrival in the region of non-Native traders, usually from the Hudson's Bay Company. Marking the beginning of significant socioeconomic change through trade and an increase in resource extraction, early contact also eventually included other cultural changes. Though fur trapping was the initial impetus for the arrival of the first settler-traders, the later discovery and lure of gold is inexorably the primary driver of changes in local populations and culture.

Non-Native settlements began to coalesce in the central-eastern Interior when traders first arrived after the 1867 transfer of Alaska from the Russian Empire to the United States, which followed the construction of the trading post of Fort Yukon in the Yukon Flats a generation earlier, in 1847. The presence of Fort Yukon—established by the Hudson's Bay Company—provided not only a permanent base of operations for settlers, who were few in number, but also a market for their activities.

The fur trapping and selling activities of these first settlers, including British and French Canadians and Europeans, paved the way for other non-Natives to settle in the region, though populations remained very small through the periods of Russian and early American ownership of Alaska. (During the Russian period, when Fort Yukon was illegally established by Hudson's Bay Company from British Canada, few Russians ever reached the Yukon Flats.) Only a very few settlers came to the south and east of Fort Yukon, in the vicinity of Central, Circle, and Eagle, and most did not remain in the area permanently.

Francois Mercier, a trader based in Fort Yukon in 1873, writes in his journal that the first prospectors had recently crossed over the Chilkoot Mountains (Mercier 1986, 26). They were four prospectors working for a man named Arthur Harper. The men arrived at Fort Yukon and started prospecting for gold, followed later by other pioneer prospectors (Osgood 1971, 8; Webb 1985, 59–60). In addition to extending their hospitality, early traders helped the prospectors by giving them work when prospecting results were discouraging (Mercier 1986, 28; Webb 1977, 61). Likewise, most food was acquired through trade with the Gwich'in and Hän Athabascans of the region, who hunted meat for trade with outsiders, and an economy of interdependency was established.

Only when the gold rushes brought in many people were the communities established that have survived up to this day, including Central, Circle, Eagle, and Fairbanks. Trading posts were instrumental in this development, as they opened doors to other newcomers by offering them hospitality and served as a sort of safety net for early travelers. Though the trading post at Fort Yukon was the earliest and most enduring, many others (including Central House—i.e., Central, Alaska) were established as economic opportunities and needs demanded. The frontier traders served an important role in the history of gold exploration and later, by supplying the tens of thousands of people who came into the country to seek their fortunes.

Other than the non-Native trappers, the miners were the first settlers to seek out a living in Alaska's central-eastern Interior. Miners formed the basis for most early non-Native settlements, and other industries and infrastructures emerged to cater to their needs. Gold exploration began when the first prospectors became curious about the land, which held promises for gold and other opportunities similar to those formerly available in the American West. A generation after the discovery of gold in California, and a generation before the discovery of gold in the Klondike, a few prospectors traveled the rivers of Interior Alaska, the eastern portion of which was made more accessible due to the presence of Fort Yukon and the Yukon River to the north and the Chilkoot Pass to the southeast (long used by indigenous peoples before its use as a mining trail to the Klondike). One of these prospectors was Anglican missionary Robert McDonald, who first discovered gold in the area, perhaps on Preacher Creek, a tributary of Birch Creek.

The arrival of prospectors (and eventually their families) was the beginning of significant changes in the region's population and was inextricably tied to the foundation and history of Central. The history of Central and the central-eastern Interior of Alaska is very much an ethnohistory of gold mining, and the first discoveries of gold were made in the mid-1880s along tributaries of the Fortymile River. Soon after, additional discoveries were made in the area that became known as the Birch Creek Mining District, which was renamed the Circle Mining District. These finds were sufficient to draw in other prospectors.

Miners fanned out across the land and made gold discoveries on many of the tributaries of nearby Birch Creek. Gus Williams, John McLeod, and Henry Lewis—already successful miners—rediscovered gold at Pavaloff and Cherosky's original discovery site of 1893 as recorded in the Sam Dunham report (1898) on Birch Creek. Half of the town of Forty Mile departed to the diggings around Birch Creek about 240 miles away. Men worked as partners, and one half would stay at the Forty Mile claim while the other went to the Circle area to try their luck (Walden 1928, 67). Hundreds of prospectors were combing the area for gold, hoping to make their fortune. They made their way up and down the Yukon River and then had to cross at least fifty miles of swampy muskeg to reach the various creeks.

Soon, discoveries quickly followed one another. By 1894, discoveries were made at Mastodon Creek, Squaw Creek, and Deadwood Creek. Due to the rapidly increasing number of prospectors in the region, the miners met together on July 22, 1894, and established Birch Creek Mining District #1 (Cook 2010), marking the first form of recorded law and order in the area. Later in July, Birch Creek Mining District #2 was established on Independence Creek. In September 1894, Eric Herman and William T. Fee discovered gold on Deadwood Creek, known at the time as Hogum Creek. According to Alfred Cook, some people filed numerous claims to tie up the creek: "they hogged 'um up" (Cook 2010). This was rectified in spring 1895, when a new recorder was appointed and changed how the claims were managed. The first miners' meeting on Deadwood Creek took place in September 1894. In 1895, gold was discovered on Eagle Creek, Harrison Creek, and Boulder Creek, and soon after it was discovered that all the creeks that flow from Mastodon Dome had gold in them. The Birch Creek Mining District later came to be called the Circle Mining District, known to the present day to be one of the most important mining districts in Alaska. Thus, in 1894, a community emerged around the roadhouse known as Central House, the origin of today's community of Central.

The Larsens/Olsons: Family History as Local Ethnohistory

Like Isaac Juneby in Eagle and Albert Carroll in Circle, the Olson family of Central represents an important source of the ethnohistory of the community and region. Through the experiences and accounts of the Olsons and Larsens, a picture is formed of resilience and adaptation in an unfamiliar environment in a foreign land. Dependency on the region's land and waters becomes a necessity, particularly in the earlier years of settlement before the establishment of even basic supply infrastructures. In such situations, settler families became dependent on one another, and often on Alaska Native people. In contrast to the point of view of a local indigenous person such as Isaac Juneby or Albert Carroll, the ethnohistory of Central is necessarily related through the eyes of settler families and their descendants, and the Olson and Larsen families characterize this experience well, beginning with the initial arrival of the Larsen brothers, Oscar, Einar, and Thorvald. Oscar's daughter, Ruth Larsen Olson, is one of the women whose life is deeply intertwined

Figure 23. A sluice box used in placer mining. (US Geological Survey, Public Domain)

with the history of Central. Her family has resided in the Central area for more than four generations and maintained a cabin there until 2015. Their family story typifies the lure of gold and the attraction it held on people from all walks of life.

The Larsen brothers came to Central from Norway, attracted by the lure of gold and the expectation of a better way of life. In the late 1800s and early 1900s, mining in the area was primarily an individual or a partnership activity using simple tools such as gold pans, sluice boxes, and rockers. Leaving the rest of their families in Norway, together Oscar, Einar, and Thorwald established a placer mine in the Birch Creek Mining District.

Placer mining methods consist of clearing the vegetation and moss from the ground, then working down to the bedrock. The gold must be separated from the gravel by moving the gravel through a sluice box using water. The water and gravel run over riffles in the sluice box to allow the gold, which is heavier than water and rocks, to drop into the bottom of the box while the waste material runs out the end. The specific mining method used depends on the ground one has to work with, the type of vegetation and how deep it is to bedrock, how much money

Figure 24. River steamer *Casca* on the Yukon River ca. 1930. (Circle District Historical Society)

needs to be invested, the amount of water necessary, and the quality of gold to be found. Due to the geological processes surrounding gold deposits, gold is not distributed evenly in the ground, and in the central-eastern Interior of Alaska it can be found concentrated on the old streambeds of the creeks.

Settlers' dependence on the transportation infrastructure is highly significant, and its profound effect on people's daily lives is reflected in the Larsen family saga. Oscar had left his wife, Eli, in Norway when he first traveled to Central. Once he had established a mining operation and built a house, Oscar decided to return to Norway and then bring Eli back to join him at his claims on Deadwood Creek. They arrived back in the United States too late in the fall to catch the last steamer of the season north to Alaska, so Oscar traveled without Eli down the Yukon River in a small boat while she spent her first winter in North Dakota with other family members. The following spring, Eli traveled via sternwheeler to Circle then by horse-and-buggy with a man who worked for Nels Rasmussen, a partner of her husband's. She eventually arrived at the

Figure 25. Ruth Larsen, age four, at "22 Above" gold discovery, Deadwood, ca. 1919. (Olson Family Collection, Circle District Historical Society)

Central Roadhouse, where Oscar met her and brought her to a prepared cabin on Deadwood Creek.

Eventually, Eli became pregnant. With the intention of heading to the closest hospital, she traveled to Circle City by wagon, where she caught the first sternwheeler that passed on the Yukon River. It happened to be headed southeast upriver to Dawson, rather than northwest and downriver to Fort Yukon, so her daughter, Ruth, was born in Dawson City, Canada.

Eli returned to Deadwood, where she and Ruth reunited with Oscar and the rest of the family. Ruth spent her early years around the gold mines located on nearby Deadwood and Switch Creeks, where her father prospected and mined with his brothers. When Ruth was a young girl, the miners on the creek would play with her and taught her to play cards. Her Uncle Einar was a very good carpenter who built her a small sluice

Figure 26. Hydraulic mining on Switch Creek, 1918 or 1928. (Olson Family Collection, Circle District Historical Society)

box with riffles that mirrored the placer-mining activities around her. She began her own "mining" operation in imitation of her father and his partners. She would "clean up" often to find nuggets and flakes of gold the other miners put in her box.

When the ground was rich in gold and prices good, the simple rocker box or gold-panning methods provided the miner a decent income and even made some people rich. When the ground was poor in gold, results were not enough to sustain a person, and additional jobs had to be taken or more effort had to be put into prospecting. Improvements in mining methods also increased the potential for profit, and thus new innovations were often quickly adopted. Oscar, Einar, and Thorwald mined in a variety of ways over the years, including hydraulic techniques, on multiple creeks, and formed partnerships with other miners.

Changing techniques made otherwise inaccessible or low-value deposits more enticing, and some of the newer claims on the creeks

Figure 27. Current remains of water diversion ditches seen from the Steese Highway used to supplement water supply for hydraulic mining. (Photo by L. Tyrrell)

around Central were located at the upper ends of the creek beds, where there was not much water to use for sluicing. Ditches were dug to divert the neighboring creeks around the hillside to supplement the water supply. At the headwaters, a system of earthen ditches and reservoirs allowed the water pressure to increase as it ran downhill. This water could be released and channeled into a pipe called a "giant," allowing a miner to use the power of gravity on flowing water to strip the overburden or move a large amount of dirt into a sluice box. This method was known as hydraulic mining, and the remains of the extensive channels can still be seen in hills of the Circle Mining District today. The Larsen/Olson family used this method for mining on their claims on Switch Creek.

Hydraulic techniques using ditch systems supplemented other mining methods, and once a hydraulic system of pipes or earthen ditches was set up, it was relatively cheap to maintain and operate. According to an article in the *Fairbanks Daily Times* in February 1908, a man named "Cow" Miller, a brother of Frank Miller who ran Miller House, was contracted to haul hydraulic mining equipment from Circle City to Eagle Creek. It took him more than one hundred days to haul the 140 tons of equipment, food, and lumber with teams of horses to the mining sites.

The Larsens' long-term presence in the region, along with others who did not depart with the bulk of the miners (often referred to as old-timers), led to their having considerable influence on the local culture, becoming historical figures and respected community members. The old-timers were the people who stayed in the region for various reasons, whether it was for the enchantment of individuality and self-sufficiency or because they felt like they did not fit into society. Some joined the other gold rushes but returned to work on their stable claims, hoping to strike it rich one day.

Clues to some of the reasons why these men and their families remained can be found in an interview with Jane Williams.[1] Jane served the Circle District Historical Society as archivist for many years and was extremely knowledgeable about and interested in the history of the Central community. During the 1950s, Jane was the community postmaster, knew all the area residents, and was a notable storyteller herself. She tells of a miner called Jens Langlow (a partner of Oscar Larsen and his daughter Ruth Larsen Olson), who would come into the post office with a little sack of gold, which were his findings for the year. Despite his meager income, there was a sparkle in his eyes and he would say in his thick, Norwegian-accented English, "Next year I vill make it, Yane." But each year there were obstacles, such as not having enough rainfall for doing the cleanup, which required much water running through the sluice boxes to separate gold from muck. And as fate would have it, the day Langlow was buried and they dug his grave, "it rained, and it rained, and it rained." They buried him in a foot of water and Jane remarked, "He would have been tickled to

---

1   Jane Williams and two others did extensive research on the trails and roadhouses of the area and the establishment of the Steese Highway. Being interested in preserving the history of the area, Jane and her husband, Red, were instrumental in the creation of Circle District Historical Society and a place to store, explore, and display relics of the past. The museum, located in Central, was the outcome of this passion. During the initial writing of this manuscript, Jane spoke with the authors many times and ensured its accuracy to the best of her knowledge. Jane was a fine storyteller and had many tales to relate about the inhabitants of the Central community, the Arctic Circle Hot Springs, and the areas inhabited up and down the creeks.

pieces, because at last he got his water" (Williams 1995). Even an elusive hope of finding gold was enough to encourage some people to continue.

The drive to discover gold (and especially to strike it rich) is documented by another prospector, James A. Carroll (the father of Albert Carroll of Circle, discussed previously), who eventually settled in the region permanently, marrying into a Gwichyaa Gwich'in family. James writes how he came to Alaska, being "seventeen years old and full of ambitious ideas about getting rich quick in Alaska and going back home to enjoy my wealth. This was forty-six years ago," he continues, and explains, "I am still waiting to overtake that pot of gold" (Carroll 1957, 11). Sometimes a dream of striking a rich claim on the mother lode was enough to sustain a person's interest, but perhaps it only was a rationalization, whereas a love of the land and the lifestyle was the real motivation.

Ruth Larsen Olson spoke of her father's love of the way of life:

Dad loved mining, and the years he had to spend away from it because of Mother's health were hard for him to endure. He could spend hours panning, and was always optimistic about the next season. Many times his optimism was all that sustained him, as some years were pretty lean, but we always had plenty of food and other necessities. (Olson 1996, 3)

Nevertheless, the mining life was difficult and often unprofitable, and in the early days, much work was performed without machinery or with only limited access to machinery. This did not prevent miners and other settlers from working toward their goals, however, due in large part to the innovative self-sufficiency that often characterized local people.

Demonstrating the importance of self-sufficiency due to the limited dependability of the transportation infrastructure, the Larsen/Olson family tales contain many stories of hunting caribou and moose, and the reliance of the newer settlers on the skills and knowledge of the indigenous inhabitants. Ruth wrote down one story for the Circle District Historical Society Museum when she was living in Central (she lived there with her husband, Roy, from 1974 to 1982). This humorous tale of her mother Eli's early years on the creek was passed down through at least three generations within the family.

Mother's first meeting with an Indian was a disaster, both for her and for the young Indian, Nathaniel. Dad had forgotten to tell Mother that he often bought moose meat from the Indians in the fall, and they would bring it to the cabin. Without warning, she opened the door when someone knocked, and there stood this young Indian boy. She screamed and slammed the door, as she had heard or read stories of Indian raids in the early days of the American settlers. The poor fellow was as startled as she was and ran up to where Dad was working and said, "Oscar, there is a woman in your cabin. I scare her, she scare me, and she scream and slam the door." Dad said, "That is my wife, and I will go back to the cabin with you and tell her you are my friend, and she won't be afraid." However, the boy refused, and walked farther away from the cabin, and I never heard if Dad got the moose meat, but I doubt it. They did not see Nathaniel again until 1922 when we were leaving Circle to go "outside" and were on the steamer *Yukon* going upriver. A young Indian came aboard and handed Mother a package. He said, "Remember me, Mrs. Larsen? I scared you on Deadwood a long time ago. My wife made this for you as a present." It was a beautiful moose-hide beaded bag, and Mother treasured it, especially for the fact that Nathaniel gave it to her. (Olson n.d., 2, 3)

The town of Deadwood, located on Deadwood Creek, where Ruth spent her childhood, has been fully abandoned. Nevertheless, the legacies of the families and individuals whose presence and activities color the local history continue to be remembered by people from the area and their descendants, enabling the reconstruction of culture-histories. Though small in population today, Central and the other settlements of the central-eastern Interior continue to bear the historical legacy of the miners and other settlers who arrived and sometimes remained for the rest of their lives.

Gold Mining and the Development of Local Culture

Without gold, there would be no community of Central, and almost every person in the region, including local Gwichyaa Gwich'in Athabascans

Figure 28. Olson family near Deadwood, July 11, 1930. In the back row are Oscar Larsen, his wife, Eli, and then Ruth Larsen. Second from the left in the front row is Einar, and the man with the tie is Big Nick Knudsen. (The Olson Family Collection, Circle District Historical Society)

(Dené), was involved in supporting the gold industry. Whether cutting wood for transportation in the form of steamships and powering gold-mining equipment, moving goods from roadhouse to community to roadhouse, or prospecting and mining along the creeks of the region, gold drove the economy and defined the motivations of most settlers. With the arrival of so many in such a short period of time, government mining authorities arrived to impose order.

Birch Creek Mining District authorities allowed for the establishment of only one claim per miner in the district. The system of staking claims and legally recording them on the creeks was also in flux, as the law changed and the system of naming the claims seemed to vary by creek. When there was no formal measuring apparatus available, the measurement used to establish a claim was pacing (measurement by walking). The discoverer of gold on the creek would stake his claim and it would be known as "discovery." The first claims upstream from there became known as "one above discovery" and the first claim below as "one below discovery." Laws regulated claim length, but because the measuring was not consistent, latecomers tended to find sections of claims that were legally too long. These became known as "fractions" that might be above or below the claims already above and below the initial discovery: "Fraction above 4 above Discovery." Then, too, "claims were often referenced to places other than a discovery claim. Reference points included discovery, upper discovery, lower discovery, discovery tree, blaze tree, mouth of creek and confluence with a tributary" (Cook 2010).

One of these gold creeks—Crooked Creek—runs through the current community of Central and divides into Porcupine and Mammoth Creeks. Mammoth Creek divides into Mastodon and Independence Creeks. The miners traveled along the Yukon River to Circle, then traveled overland and inland to the goldfields. Crooked Creek flows into Birch Creek at a location known as Jumpoff, which was named for being the farthest point one could navigate to up Birch Creek from the Yukon River. From there, the miners jumped off the river systems and crossed the country. As the miners needed food and supplies to work their claims, roadhouses and stores (trading posts) grew up to provide them with necessary materials and some forms of comfort.

Consequently, increasing numbers of prospectors encouraged the traders to move trading posts away from the Native settlements and establish their posts near the gold-bearing creeks. With the great influx of both miners and resources, traders could profit easily by supplying miners' needs; in the social climate of the time, obliging Native people to come to the posts' new locations was not an issue. By then, a dependency on manufactured goods and processed foods was emerging, and trade continued between indigenous people and settlers, though increasingly to the disadvantage of the indigenous traders. Trading posts further attracted other service providers, including, of course, saloons.

During the rapid growth of towns, saloons and dance halls also offered some warmth as social settings, and people would make the effort to visit and gather together using almost any excuse for an event whenever something fun was happening. As Ruth Larsen Olson remembers, in the early to mid-twentieth century, there were dances and holiday celebrations, and many people played a musical instrument. Ruth described how people would hike considerable distances to attend parties in places like Miller House or Arctic Circle Hot Springs. They would dress in their fancy suits and walking boots, put their dancing shoes in a backpack, and hike to the party (Olson 1996). The locations and presence of these establishments, however, changed frequently as people moved around according to the needs of the mining operations.

Due to the instability of populations, many names and places were in flux in the late 1800s and early 1900s, as people relocated with the gold discoveries and as opportunities for employment changed. These often-ephemeral communities, some described below, nevertheless usually constituted the source of the settlers of the next community to be established for mining or woodcutting. In addition to these earlier-established settlers were many new arrivals, often from other waning mining efforts in the northwestern regions of North America, though many came from a wide variety of rural and urban backgrounds, from across the continent, and sometimes from Europe as well. As a result of this constant change, populations fluctuated greatly, especially with the discovery of gold to the east in what would become the Yukon Territory (1898) in the Klondike River and its tributaries. Towns grew up at Circle Hot Springs, Miller House, and Deadwood. Records for Mastodon, Independence, and Deadwood Creeks are still in existence, but the early records for Squaw Creek and Harrison Creek disappeared as the claims and creeks were abandoned during the Klondike gold rush (1896–1899). These places were re-staked in 1897 as new miners arrived or others returned to the region.

The discovery of the Klondike River's gold emptied mining areas around Circle and the Fortymile River. The people who already were in the vicinity of the Klondike were in a favorable position and, in effect, they staked the best claims before people from outside the region had the chance to do so. As Melody Webb writes, the best claims were staked long before the steamboat *Excelsior* arrived at San Francisco, bearing the news of promising finds (Webb 1985, 123). More important is that after the initial excitement of the Klondike had waned, many of the American miners returned to the Alaska side of the border. They returned first to the creeks near the border, exploring and prospecting, and some flowed back to the Circle Mining District as well (Webb 1985, 133–134). Returning American miners also established new towns, such as Eagle City in 1897–1898, and started mining operations on Mission and American Creeks. Star City was established in the same year on the left bank of the Yukon, some thirty miles below Mission Creek (Osgood 1971, 12), and towns like Ivy City and Nation City at the mouth of the Nation River also sprang up. Webb suggests that many of the patriotic names, such as Fourth of July Creek and American Creek, reflected the general relief of the miners who came back to American soil. While not key to the story of the community of Central, this reflects the amount of people, goods, and materials that traveled through the region. In later years, the people who were living at the creeks were divided between those who considered their nearest town to be Circle and those who frequented Eagle, and these two communities have been socially linked ever since.

During the heyday of the settler towns in the central-eastern Interior (ca. 1895–1945), they served populations of people who did not actually live in any of the towns and who did not necessarily identify with the settlements. This mirrors the settlement patterns of miners who, though dependent on the towns for provisions, would frequently relocate to prospect elsewhere (though some did remain for extended periods and were considered a part of the extended settlement community). Carolyn Kelly's oral history interview from 1991 provides an example. Kelly was one of the back-to-the-landers[2] of the 1970s, and according to her, the Kandik River was the mental borderline for the people of Eagle, who did not often extend their travels any farther downriver (Kelly 1991).

But it was in no small way the roadhouses established throughout the region that tied the towns and their people together, and to the miners living and working on their claims, and so regional links were established and maintained for practical reasons. Roadhouses provided food and lodging, entertainment, and social opportunities to the miners and traders who lived in and moved through the region. They also enabled safer and easier travel between communities, and their presence along the trails and roads was central to the emergence of sustainable communities and

---

2   The back-to-the-landers were a population of unrelated settlers who in the 1970s came to parts of Alaska to live off the land in isolation from greater society for a variety of reasons (McPhee 1976). Though most would later depart, some few remain to the present.

mining operations, especially in the early years of the late nineteenth to early twentieth centuries.

The Role of Roadhouses in Local Development

While many miners and other settlers rushed to new areas, a small population remained to mine the creeks where they knew there was gold rather than risk highly competitive prospecting in richer grounds. In order to attend to the frequent influx and outflow of miners, services such as freighting mining equipment, roadhouses, and mail delivery developed in the region. Arthur T. Walden describes his freighting using dogsleds beginning in the winter of 1896. He would pick up freight left in Circle City from one of the three steamships plying the Yukon River and cross the sixty-five to eighty miles to the Birch Creek diggings by sled. "The trail across was over a swampy plateau covered with shallow ponds and muskeg, and a few stunted spruces. In the summer there was absolutely no game of any kind on these flats on account of the mosquitoes, which are simply impossible to describe" (Walden 1928, 26). During the winter, five different people made it their entire business to haul the freight by dogs out to the mines, Walden being one of them. There were two way houses that had taverns attached to accommodate overnight travelers, and corrals were specially constructed to keep the dog mushers' sleds in and the dogs out. These way houses were critical to the provisioning of miners and others who worked the surrounding country, and most were local centers of culture and community in addition to being temporary stopovers.

The way houses later became known as roadhouses. One of these was the Grand Central Way House—the kernel of the community of Central. The settlement of Central began with the building of the Grand Central Way House around 1894 to serve the supply trail between the Yukon River at Circle and the mines at Mammoth, Mastodon, Preacher, and Birch Creeks. Miners and others settled around Central House, which was situated at the crossing of Crooked Creek, to engage themselves in the supply of food, shelter, and equipment to nearby active miners (Ordway 2010). Its importance and population fluctuated as the years passed, as did the

Figure 29. Horses and sleds in Central-Circle area. Big Nick Knudsen with Jens Langlow standing. (The Olson Family Collection, Circle District Historical Society)

mining activity in the area. During the years of increased mining activity or due to the establishment of equipment that required wood for power, more people would remain to cut and gather wood during the winter months. As with Isaac Juneby's family (see chapter 2) and Albert Carroll's family (see chapter 3), sometimes this work was conducted by Alaska Natives.

By 1906, a pack trail with a steady stream of summer and winter activity ran from Circle on the Yukon River through Central House to the mining operations on upper Birch Creek. During the summers of 1906 and 1907, the pack trail was upgraded to a wagon road, and by 1908 it went through Central as far as Miller House, leading to an increase in the number of active mines in the region. The Reiger family even moved their roadhouse, which would later be known as Ferry, so it would be on the trail. By this time, mining companies on Mammoth Creek used a steam shovel, attracting more settlers seeking employment as wood-cutters or machine operators. Prospector Clarence "C. J." Berry began staking and buying claims on nearby Eagle Creek sometime in 1906 and began to use hydraulic methods (see below) as early as 1907.

The first wave of prospectors may have been mostly men, but women, too, saw opportunities on the gold rush frontier of Alaska. They were determined to make their own fortunes, for example, as camp cooks, laundresses, or bakers. Due to the values and morals of the day, oftentimes these women would not have been considered "respectable" in the eyes of their peers. As Frances Blackhouse (1995) suggests, women enjoyed the lax social codes of the gold towns, which gave them much more freedom than they ever had in the Victorian-age societies from which many of them originated. Some women traveled with their husbands, or their husbands sent for them after a cabin had been built and some forms of comfort had been put in place. Soon after the establishment of the basic infrastructure such as roads, roadhouses, and supply networks, women and children arrived with increasing frequency, and families became the center of community stability and character.

Mining as Culture-History in the Circle Mining District

It is important to note that in spite of declining interest, mining has continued in the area. Even during the gold rushes to places like Nome and Tanana, some miners stubbornly continued working on their claims in the central-eastern Interior, although no new bonanzas were found (Beckstead 2003, 3). There were more than seventy mines that employed 256 men in the Eagle-Circle area between 1915 and 1916 (Webb 1985, 283). The bulk of the population was changing constantly, as people were flowing in and out of the area, but there were also those, like the Larsens/Olsons, who stayed throughout the years. Those who did remain witnessed and at times participated in the great changes that occurred in mining over the decades since the arrival of settlers, representing an ongoing readjustment of labor and settlement patterns.

Early-Twentieth-Century Changes in Mining and Local Culture

Mining underwent important changes at the beginning of the twentieth century but continued to be the main economic activity of Central. The changes in mining happened for multiple reasons. First, the easily mined gold deposits were quickly exhausted, and more dirt had to be processed for sufficient payment. Second, technological developments made processing dirt easier. Third, economic conditions surrounding gold prices have always affected miners, and gold mining was less likely to be seen as an attractive possibility if the prices were low.

Changing mining techniques, however, were not the only cause of demographic shifts in the Circle Mining District and in Central. During World War I, a depression in the gold market occurred, causing a contraction in mining activity. The war depleted the available labor supply and raised the price of materials and equipment, as well as the cost of transportation. Still, individual miners and larger mining companies invested in the gold capability of the area, and hydraulic methods were employed on Mastodon Creek, Eagle Creek, and Switch Creek.

In about 1911, a new mining innovation made its appearance in the area: the dredge. A dredge is a large piece of equipment situated on a barge that must have enough water to float as it moves along the valley floor. A line of buckets digs into the gravel back and forth across the valley floor. The barge is tied to winches moored to the shore on each side that allow it to advance. The buckets dump onto a conveyor belt, then into a revolving washer to be dropped into the sluice box, washed with water, then placed onto a conveyor and moved out the backside of the dredge, leaving distinctive conical crescent-shaped piles as the stacker sweeps side to side.

Dredging was highly effective, and according to Douglas Beckstead (2003), even a small dredge was capable of digging approximately five hundred cubic yards of earth a day, whereas a single miner on a hand-mined claim could process one cubic yard a day. Sluice boxes and other small-scale equipment could also increase efficiency (Beckstead 2003, 69). Increased dirt-processing capacity made it economically viable to continue mining low-grade deposits, and the era of one-man claims was coming to an end, although partnerships and family-operated claims continue to the present.

Dredges required a large investment for the machinery itself and also required hiring a crew, and this necessarily changed the economic organization and labor patterns of the region. Though more settlers than indigenous people worked in this changing economic condition, Alaska Natives were present in the area and in the industry, if in small numbers. Labor was characterized by wages more so than in the past, and only the most persistent could maintain competitive small-scale operations not reliant

Figure 30. Dredge in the Central-Circle area. (Frank and Mary Warren Collection, Circle District Historical Society)

on heavy machinery. The men working the dredges in the area would be laid off during the fall, as the freezing temperatures shut down the operations until spring returned. Some remained and cut wood for the steam engines and supplemented their income with trapping. Miners overwintering at Arctic Circle Hot Springs or in Central itself supplemented their income in this manner. Others would take themselves and their families and leave on the last steamer available; other families might leave to provide an education for their children or to get medical treatment during the long winter months.

The lure of gold and other opportunities did not abate, and dredges increasingly appeared on many of the area creeks. In the winter of 1911, a dredge was floated from near Dawson to Circle City, then hauled overland by teams of horses during the winter to be reassembled on Mastodon Creek, where it operated during 1912 and 1913. A couple of the buckets from this dredge were later relocated to the Circle Mining District Historical Museum in Central many years after the dredge was

Figure 31. Berry Dredge on Mammoth Creek, 1937. (Dan and Esther Bergevin Collection, Circle District Historical Society)

Figure 32. The Berry House at Miller House. (Frank and Mary Warren Collection, Circle District Historical Society)

abandoned. Between 1915 and 1916, a new steam-powered dredge was built on Mammoth Creek. Operated by the Berry Dredging Company, it mined along Mammoth Creek, then along Mastodon Creek.

Clarence Berry, who founded the Berry Dredging Company, came north in 1894 and was one of the few Klondike prospectors who became a millionaire. He acquired claims on Mammoth, Mastodon, and Eagle Creeks in 1906 that are still producing to this day. He has been credited as being the first miner to use a steam point in thawing the ground ahead of mining.

As is evident, building the necessary infrastructure required capital that could only be accumulated by a large company. Therefore, companies were formed, and after careful prospecting they started consolidating individual mining claims by buying out old-timers (Beckstead 2003, 4). During 1922, the Berry dredge was reassembled on Mammoth Creek and operated on Mammoth, Mastodon, and Independence Creeks until 1926.

In 1932, the price of gold rose from $20.67 an ounce to $35 an ounce. In the heart of the region, Gold Placers, Inc. had prospected at Coal Creek, finding a place for a dredge. They bought out the old-timers, and in 1935 they brought in a dredge. A flourishing operation emerged that brought along with it a postal service and improvements in transportation (Beckstead 2003, 104–105). Coal Creek (where the Junebys and others from Eagle worked and lived) and Woodchopper Creek dredges ran successfully until the 1960s, when they finally closed. They had provided work for many local families as well as for outsiders, and left a permanent mark in the history of the central-eastern Interior. Now the old dredge can be visited at Coal Creek.

All this work and accomplishment was ultimately dependent on the transportation system that carried supplies and people in and out of Alaska, and the disruption of the system could be difficult on settler populations. On October 18, 1918, a tragedy befell the region as a steamer, the *Princess Sophia*, struck the Vanderbilt Reef between Skagway and Juneau, knocking a hole in the ship during a snowstorm. According to Ken Coates and Bill Morrison, when the *Princess Sophia* sank (around October 26), it took the lives of a "cross section of northern society miners, businessmen, civil

Figure 33. Internal machinery of the gold dredge at Coal Creek. (Photo by L. Tyrrell)

servants, steam boatmen, their wives and children" (Coates and Morrison 1990, xii). Not only did the event claim the lives of all 353 passengers and crew, but it "dealt an almost lethal blow" to the mining districts of the far northwest (Coates and Morrison 1990, xii), which relied upon these ships for transportation and food supply. Local residents were personally affected: according to Ruth Larsen Olson, as many as thirteen people from the creeks and mines surrounding Central were aboard the *Princess Sophia* when it sank, including Mr. and Mrs. Garner, who ran the dredging and other mining operations on Eagle Creek.

The Great Depression and World War II:
Local Stability, Local Decline

Small-scale mining operations did not become extinct, however, and small-scale mining and commercial trapping continued to be sources of income for many people. During the great depression of the 1930s, gold prices were still high, and unemployed people started mining even though investments in large operations could not be made (Webb 1985, 284). In Central and the Hot Springs, it was common to supplement mining income by trapping during the winter, cutting wood, and providing meat for oneself and others through hunting activities.

Ernest Patty began dredging operations at Coal Creek during 1934, providing more local employment options. By 1940, the Circle Mining District had produced $1.5 million in gold (Webb 1977, 286). Dredges were operating at Coal Creek, Woodchopper, Deadwood, and Mammoth Creek as well. The US entry into World War II halted all mining efforts, as the government decreed that gold mining was a nonessential industry. Equipment and manpower were diverted to other areas, resulting in some outmigration from the region. The boom-and-bust cycle continues to play out, with more miners and mines operating when the price of gold is higher and finding employment elsewhere when the price falls. So, too, do the lots of the stores, bars, hotels, freighters, mechanics, fuel haulers, and other jobs that provide services to the miners rise and fall as this economic fluctuation occurs.

The Postwar Resurgence

After World War II, mining resurged. In 1948, Berry dredge's steam engines were replaced with new diesel engines, and the dredge continued to operate intermittently with various owners until it burned near the mouth of Bedrock Creek. Some miners returned to the area after the war, but mining operations were much reduced compared to prewar times, and mining continued to decline through the 1950s and 1960s. In 1957, Ernest Patty closed his operation at Coal Creek and Woodchopper, and many, including the Junebys, returned to Eagle, Central, or Circle.

In 1967, the fixed standard on gold was removed, and the price of gold rose.[3] Despite the fact that there had been active mining in the

---

3   Until 1968, the US dollar represented a fixed amount of gold. For every dollar in circulation, the US government had gold to back it up. Dollars were convertible to gold at a price fixed by the US Treasury. From 1934 to 1967, that fixed price was $35 per ounce.

central-eastern Interior for more than one hundred years and the rich deposits had been mined away, many people started small-time mining when gold prices rose in the 1970s. Miners were staking claims on all the area creeks and mining activity increased substantially; by 1978, the Circle Mining District was the most active in Alaska, with sixty-five gold-mining operations employing more than two hundred people (ACDO). There was also an attempt to revive operations on the Yukon at Coal Creek, between Circle and Eagle, when Ernie Wolff and Dan Colben bought the old dredge from Alluvial Gold and hired a crew of local people, in addition to outsiders, to run it (Juneby 2010). According to Ray Bell (1991), it started running again in 1977 but didn't make any profit, and the operation was abandoned soon afterward.

Fluctuating markets have long been a feature of resource extraction, and small-scale operations are nevertheless the hardest hit economically when gold prices drop and markets shrink. More so than in other areas, the Circle Mining District, with the community of Central at its cultural center, exists as a result of the presence and activities of small-scale miners, representing an industrial-age activity that nevertheless almost always occurs in rural areas and has a long-established set of mining-related customs and traditions, as well as an ongoing interdependency with one another and with local communities. With connection to the local land and water, the people who bear these customs develop a local identity that permanently ties them to the community of Central and the Circle Mining District.

Late-Twentieth-Century Decline and Early-Twenty-First-Century Growth

A reduction in mining activities followed the boom of the 1970s and 1980s. As mentioned earlier, in 1978 President Jimmy Carter proclaimed fifty-six million acres of Alaska as national monuments. The creation of the Yukon–Charley Rivers National Preserve in 1980 suddenly and severely limited the activities allowed inside the area. Now the people in Circle, Central, and Eagle were not allowed to participate in many of the activities they were accustomed to as a means of earning a living, such as trapping and woodcutting. Cabins required permits, boats required current registrations, and miners required permission to access their mines. Residents of all three communities, and places in between, have chafed against the new and more numerous regulations governing their activities.

US National Park Service employees and residents have interacted repeatedly, as people continue their subsistence activities in the federally designated land that surrounds these communities. Small incidents with negative overtones pile on top of other tense interactions, leading to a local impression that residents are unwelcome in the Yukon–Charley Rivers National Preserve but visitors are made comfortable. Some residents have dealt with this feeling by moving their subsistence activities elsewhere, while others have been involved in outright confrontations as they insist on their perceived rights. Unsurprisingly, the National Park Service has more often than not prevailed within the state and federal court systems, leaving local residents feeling disregarded and oppressed. It should be noted that some employees of the park service, usually locals or longtime residents, are empathetic and compassionate to local concerns and conditions and try to intercede to foster good relations. But to demonstrate this sometimes-strained relationship, a few case examples can be noted.

Joe Vogler, an old-timer, lawyer, and gold miner, had claims on Ketchum Creek, close to Central. He had lived and mined in the Central area for many years and was a well-known figure at the Arctic Circle Hot Springs restaurant, bar, and hotel, where he regularly met with other old-timers. He also had a patented mining claim on Woodchopper Creek that was in an area that had been set aside as part of the Yukon–Charley Rivers National Preserve. Holding strong views on the Constitution and this use of public lands, Vogler took action that resulted in a heated disagreement with the National Park Service. It became known as the Battle at Webber Creek, named after a documentary film that was made by KUAC-TV (1985).

Vogler intentionally provoked the National Park Service because he felt the Constitution of the United States protected his right to cross federal property in order to gain access to his mining claims. The park service maintained it could regulate when and where Vogler could access his claims by requiring him to apply for a permit to cross the land during the winter months, when it would entail less damage to the tundra. Vogler assembled multiple pieces of heavy mining equipment at Arctic Circle Hot Springs during the summer months. He traveled a historic trail called the Bielenburg, with Arctic Circle Hot Springs at one end and Coal Creek on the other side of Woodchopper Creek at the other end. A local family provided him with aerial support, flying over him to keep track of his progress, and let him know a federal contingent was on its way. The government sent helicopters and law enforcement with flak jackets and loaded firearms to halt his progress at Webber Creek. Vogler was very thankful that others were watching the entire incident, feeling it could have ended in a more violent manner. Crediting the pilot with saving his life, he rewarded the man with a piece of his patented claim within the Yukon–Charley Rivers—an inholding. Vogler lost the ensuing judicial battle, much to the disappointment of many Central residents, and was ordered to remove his equipment the way it had entered.

The relationship between the National Park Service and other federal regulatory agencies and the residents of the three communities has continued to be fraught with tension. The National Park Service has the power to enforce and regulate local usage, including subsistence activities, on nationally held lands. There are many stories circulated in local lore that underline the feelings of resentment harbored toward the institutions and federal bureaucracies like the National Park Service. The local viewpoint of excessive and aggressive enforcement is displayed through incidents that reflect the range of relatively minor interactions to some major face-offs, like the Vogler incident, resulting in court cases.

Two others stand out over time, one that was resolved and one that has been taken to the Supreme Court, which was discussed in chapter 2. The case of Jim Wilde, a seventy-year-old resident of Central, worked its way to resolution within the Alaska court system. In the course of his seasonal subsistence hunting activities, Jim and his fully loaded boat were stopped on the Yukon River by National Park Service rangers for a safety inspection. During this interaction, the rangers used firearms to subdue and then arrest Jim, taking him to jail in Fairbanks under cover of darkness. Jim takes great delight in the fact that his knowledge of the river was an integral part of directing the rangers, in the boat in which he was held, to the community of Circle. Without his assistance, the rangers would have missed the mouth of the slough where Circle is located. Furthermore, Jim's wife and boat were left on the banks of the Yukon to find their own way home. She had to call upon friends from Central to bring up another driver for her boat in order to get home. Locals see leaving this elderly woman alone on the shores of the Yukon River as a serious breach of etiquette perpetuated by park service rangers. Jim Wilde endured a few years of probation and was eventually fined by the courts for not having a current boat registration.

The Tyrrell family never had a major confrontation with park service employees, but due to many small incidents, they chose to move their spring bear hunting to another location. Before this area became a national preserve, they would shelter at Coal Creek or Woodchopper Creek, where there are many old empty buildings from the gold-mining activities. During late April and early May, they would move the family to some of these buildings for warmth during their black bear hunting activities. Many years, it is still snowing during this time and can be chilly at night. One year, the Tyrrells arrived to find the buildings locked, so they picked a campsite for the tent-and-tarp shelter down by the river. They were soon asked by park service employees to move their "stuff," including an airplane that was parked off the end of the runway, as it was blocking the runway, according to the park service. In the Tyrrells' view, there was plenty of room on the flattened gravel to drive the truck around the plane.

Another year, the Tyrrells brought bicycles to ride the few miles to the hills where it is easy to see the black bears eating the early grass. A park service employee sitting on a four-wheeler told the family, "No wheeled vehicles are allowed." Another year, an experiment was being conducted involving aircraft, the military, and caribou. There was a lot of noisy activity, and park service employees were riding four-wheelers all over the place, roaring up to where family members were quietly watching bears, resulting in the game being scared away. The easiest way for the Tyrrell family to deal with this increase in activity and seeming active discouragement was to move somewhere else, where there were no people. Others are not as fortunate to have this option. Such places as fishing sites for fish camps are very difficult, if not impossible, to move, but the Tyrrells were lucky that they could simply move the focus of their activities to avoid harassment.

Other changes in federally managed lands around Central began in the early part of the 1980s, when upper Birch Creek became designated as a wild river within the Wild and Scenic River system, and pressure began building to clean up the water of Birch Creek. Until this point, miners had put their sluice boxes in the streams and used the motion of the water to wash away dirt in order to extract the gold. The water was not treated in any way, and mud was not viewed as a contaminant of the creek. Regulations steadily became stricter. Environmental groups such as the Sierra Club, along with the Denduu Gwich'in people of Birch Creek Village, located downriver of the mines, sued the Bureau of Land Management for not doing enough to restrict the amount of mud the mining industry released into the water, as it sometimes fouled fish habitat. This problem was addressed, and the mining inspectors attempted to maintain a delicate regulatory balance, as explained by Bill Glanz (Glanz and Glanz 2010), who described mining inspectors who actually helped the miners: "They considered claims to be five acres even though they weren't, and didn't mind if the creek was a little bit muddy. They did everything they could to keep the creek water clean, but sometimes it was not possible. Strict restrictions kept the miners away even though the price of gold would be good."

Lori (Hannelore) Wilde elaborated (2010), explaining that the Environmental Protection Agency (EPA) changed things in an attempt to ensure clean water. At the Alaska Miners Association meeting, the EPA was resisted, and some of the restrictions were never implemented, though others passed. Although some of the streams had arsenic to begin with, the practice of using settling ponds reportedly caused the arsenic to concentrate while at the same time blocking it from the rivers. Now people are required to use settling ponds, a practice introduced in the 1970s and 1980s. Before then, settling ponds were not used except during dry summers, when the creek water was insufficient. The Bureau of Land Management also devised more restrictive regulations on the turbidity of water to be released back into the stream, and a plan calling for reclamation of the land to be carried out by miners on tailing piles was put in place.

The introduction of settling ponds and other regulatory require-ments, coupled with declining gold prices after a record high in January 1980 of $2,072.55 per ounce, led the number of active mining claims to gradually decrease in the Circle Mining District. Prices continued to decline through the 1990s, and after reaching a low point of $355.09 per ounce in March 2001, the price of gold began to rise again in the 2000s, steadily increasing in the new millennium with some fluctuations. Rising prices, coupled with the spread of phone service in areas immediately out-side Central, led to some economic revival, and Central's mining activi-ties are supplemented by a small tourist industry, formerly focused on nearby Arctic Circle Hot Springs and its small resort, which was closed in October 2002, reducing tourist revenues. The price of gold reached a high point of $1,835.05 in November 2011, and has slowly but steadily declined to the present ($1,298.85 as of this writing in September 2017).

Nevertheless, despite these fluctuations, there has been a small increase in mining activity. Earlier, high degrees of fluctuation in gold prices caused some hesitation for investment and involvement in gold mining, though the practice remains widespread throughout the central-eastern Interior of Alaska. For the last two years, price fluctuations have been historically minimal. During the summer of 2014, according to Becky Hendrickson, the postmaster in Central and an active officer in the Circle District Miners' Association, there were at least thirty different mining operations in the Central area. Currently, the price of gold is often said to be not high enough to warrant the initiation of large-scale operations, but it is high enough to be viable for small-scale endeavors.

Mining is certainly the primary, but not the only, thread of history in the makeup of the current community of Central. The existence of Arctic Circle Hot Springs, and later its hotel, had a profound effect upon the resi-dents and their wage-earning opportunities. The Arctic Circle Hot Springs Resort brought capital and cash into the community and served as a source of local economic diversification, increasing Central's economic resilience during the time of its operation. Socially and economically, the hot springs have been an important feature of Central throughout its history.

Special Topic: Arctic Circle Hot Springs

According to the *Dictionary of Alaska Place Names* (Orth 1967), Arctic Circle Hot Springs was discovered by William Greats in 1893. However, there is an oral story that relates a moose hunter, perhaps named William Hunter or William Coates, finding the springs while looking for a moose. He had wounded a moose and was following it when he found plumes of steam coming from a stream of open water. Following the stream, he found a cave-like hole in the hillside out of which issued hot water. Supposedly, he and another man came back to camp there for an extended period, making a little pool in which to soak. The medicinal benefits were a surprise to them.

Yet another source, Patricia Oakes, credits a prospector named Billy Greets with finding the hot springs in 1897, between Portage and Deadwood Creeks, while prospecting for gold (Oakes 1984). Frank Leach stated in his homesteading patent application that James Jenson, a miner on Deadwood Creek, discovered the hot springs in the fall of 1897. Regardless of who found it, it was Cassius Monohon who cut a sideline from Circle to the Mastodon Trail and set up a roadhouse and eventually obtained an eighty-acre homestead in 1905. Frank Leach obtained a 160-acre homestead in 1909 with Monohon as a witness. Eventually, with Monohon's support, Leach surveyed and patented the homestead. Leach lived and worked there and claimed that the mineralized water was highly medicinal.

According to former resident Robert Cacy (2004), Frank Leach was a highly educated man. Having attended Whitman Agricultural College in Walla Walla, Washington, he was intensely interested in hydroponics and providing plants nutrients while growing in water. Leach reportedly found relief for his arthritis in the healing water of the springs and began to recommend it as a health spa. He built small soaking pools for the miners, then a larger swimming pool. He actively encouraged miners to overwinter in the area and allowed them to build cabins on his homestead. Leach hauled topsoil, built underground drains, and used the water from the natural hot springs to heat his gardens. He began planting and cultivating a garden that reached five acres in size. The cabbages, carrots, potatoes, cauliflower, celery, and tomatoes grown there were noted to be of fantastic size and provided fresh vegetables for the miners who lived in the area and for the resort itself. During some years, the vegetables were even trucked to Fairbanks.

Leach had an encounter with a moose while brushing the lines for his homestead and ended up with a broken leg. He took a steamer down the Yukon to the Hudson Stuck Hospital at Fort Yukon. There he met, and subsequently married, Emma Gung, his nurse.

Feeling aviation was important to the future of Alaska, Leach used a horse-drawn grader to construct a 400-by-2,400-foot runway in 1924 (Oakes 1984, 37). It was touted as the first landing strip to be specifically designed for airplane traffic within the state of Alaska. In August 1924, Noel Wien and Jim Rodebaugh landed at the Circle Hot Springs airport. Since the surface of the runway was softer than expected, Frank Leach helped with a couple of horses to pull the airplane upright after landing.

When Fort Egbert in Eagle closed, Leach bought many tons of supplies, barging them down the Yukon to Circle and hauling them overland by horse and wagon to build his hotel. He also made an eight-mile road to connect to the Steese Highway (discussed in more detail below), which at the time was still under construction (Cacy 2004). As mentioned in the previous chapter, the creation of the Steese Highway represents a very significant historic shift in transportation and supply away from the Yukon River inland to the mines.

After the Steese Highway opened in 1928, Leach further expanded his homestead, and by 1930 he had built a three-and-a-half-story hotel that could accommodate more than one hundred guests. There were icehouses and greenhouses. The hotel itself was heated by the water from the hot springs through a gravity-fed system. It was known as a health resort and had a landing field, a farm, a telephone, a weather station, a US Commissioner/Recorder's office, and a post office. Miners continued to build cabins there to winter in, and the place was a center of social activity, hosting area-wide dinners and parties. The dinners featured six or seven varieties of vegetables grown in the extensive gardens and geothermally heated greenhouses. Miners and tourists soaked in log-lined swimming pools.

In 1931, a traveler by the name of Norma J. Hog wrote a letter to her mother about a trip she took to Circle and the hot springs:

> We left Circle at 7 pm (gas 65 cents [per gallon]) and drove to Hot Springs where we spent the night in a nice hotel—all heated by the water just as it comes out of the ground. It's 139°. Mr. Leach has built up a resort there but it's not well known yet. He has a dozen or more cabins all heated by this hot water. It's an ideal spot. Not so costly either considering how far away it is. It's $1 for a bed and $1 for each meal. We had a grand swim in the [unreadable] plunge and slept like logs. All the "Sourdoughs" are so interesting. We hear stories and more stories and can hardly get away from them. So many of the old-timers seem to be real intelligent men—course they read a great deal as they're in solitude for many months. Mr. Leach has a greenhouse with tomatoes and cucumbers then has a big garden of carrots, cabbages [unreadable] cows—so I had a glass of milk for breakfast as I expect I'd not get another taste of it before or until I go back to the States. It's all canned milk here. (Hog 1931)

In 1939, Frank Leach sold his interest in the hotel and concentrated solely on his gardens. He continued to provide fresh vegetables to the miners, the hotel, and Fairbanks well into the 1950s. Meanwhile, the hotel had a series of owner-operators, including Robert Cacy's mother and father in the early 1940s when he was young, and himself during the 1950s.

According to an article about the hot springs written by Roger Kaye, longtime area resident Roy Olson stated, "A decline in mining and sale of the resort in the '60s to an absentee owner looking for a tax write-off began a sad decline at the resort." Kaye (1992, 9) continues:

> The lush gardens were abandoned and the greenhouses torn down. A long series of managers neglected maintenance the old buildings required. In the late '70s the original homestead was subdivided and sold for cabin sites. Fairbanksan Bob Miller purchased the fifty-acre section that included the buildings and pool [built by John and Ruth Berdahl].

Figure 34. Arctic Circle Hot Springs hotel, upper garden, and cabins, 1940. (Dan and Esther Bergevin Collection, Circle District Historical Society)

Sinking a fortune into refurbishing the old hotel, "Bobby" Miller made major improvements. The kitchen was remodeled, as was the entire hotel. The individual miners' cabins were restored, and the Olympic-size swimming pool was given a face-lift. Miller also brought with him his salvage and surplus furniture, old ATCOs (Alberta Trading Company prefabricated housing), scrap lumber, and piles of rusty pipes. Some of the Alaska pipeline's surplus ATCOs from its construction were covered with slab wood and placed along the entrance road to the hotel to be used as living quarters for employees, or possibly as overflow guest rooms.

During the 1980s, gold drastically increased in value, and the Circle Mining District was awash with miners and their families. Robert (Bob) and Loretta LeRude began to manage the hotel and bar. The hot springs resort was once again the social gathering point for the district. The annual miner's picnic alternated with businesses in Central, but at the hot springs resort there was the hotel and cabins and the big swimming pool, all heated from the springs. Eventually, other enterprises emerged, including a bakery, a gift shop, a general store, an ice cream parlor, a laundromat, a bar and restaurant, a masseuse, a community garden, a community water hose, and greenhouses.

In 1985, Ruth and Roy Olson celebrated their fiftieth wedding anniversary at the Arctic Circle Hot Springs Resort, which had been such a part of their lives. It was said to have been one of the largest parties ever held at the springs, with folks coming from many miles away to attend.

Laverna Miller, Bobby's wife, ran the resort from 1997 until 2002. Sadly, in that year the resort closed its doors and as of this writing has not reopened, except for a short time during the fire season of 2004, when hundreds of firefighters from all over the country made their headquarters at the hot springs. The firefighters protected the community of Central from fires that burned in every direction. The closing of Arctic Circle Hot Springs resort has negatively affected the community of Central and the residents of the area, both economically and socially. The economic viability of the area is consequently uncertain.

Special Topic: Flooding in Central

In most incidents, local people endeavor to work together to solve local problems, and a frequent one is flooding. Floods seem to be a part of the natural order of things along the Yukon River and its tributaries; ice breakups tend to cause tensions and excitement every spring. There are, however, various ways of coping with floods, and they tend to pull the people of a community together. When rain starts falling in large amounts, people begin to think about preparing for disaster mitigation and relief, and working cooperatively is essential to success.

Summer thundershowers can cause the water flow in creeks and streams to increase dramatically. It is not unusual in the course of an ordinary summer thunderstorm to have the Birch Creek and its tributaries rise several feet in less than an hour, threatening any activities along the banks and cutting transportation routes until the water level drops (Oakes 1983, 3). The community of Central dealt with annual flooding by constructing a dike on Crooked Creek next to the bridge that runs through the center of town. Jane Williams has noted that Central House used to flood every year, but building the dike saved Central of this annoyance.

There are, however, a couple of floods known as hundred-year floods, which refers to flood events that do not happen each year but only once in a great while. In 1914, the old Hän settlement of Charley Village flooded, and the band dispersed into the communities of Eagle and Circle (Mishler and Simeone 2004, 105). In 1967, Birch Creek, the Chena and Tanana Rivers, and their tributaries experienced such a phenomenon, leading to a devastating flood of Fairbanks and surrounding areas. Patricia Oakes, long-term resident of Central who was an area historian, referred to it as:

> a single event which changed the courses and bank lines of the Birch and its tributaries more than anything yet observed by humanity. The massive force and flow of this flood cut and changed banks of the Birch and its tributaries along the entire watershed, opening areas previously sealed by vegetative ground cover to quick erosion from any activities since that time. During this flood, water levels were so high that the Birch overflowed its banks and flooded the Yukon Flats west of Circle City to the point that both rivers were joined and mature birch trees floated across from the Birch channel into the Yukon. (Oakes 1983, 3)

In 1984, there were flash floods that affected the miners on the area creeks. Constance Tyler (n.d.) wrote about this flood in her personal diaries. She and her husband ran a fuel business catering to area miners and repaired heavy mining equipment both in the field and at a shop they built on their lot off the Circle Hot Springs Road during the 1980s. The Environmental Protection Agency had set up new turbidity standards and permits for the miners, gold was low (fluctuating between $400 and $319 per ounce), and spring was late. All these factors joined together to make a slow, quiet season. However, the tractor business had been as busy as usual, due in part to a flood in June that damaged many miners' equipment:

> The flood affected most of the miners in the district but hit Deadwood hardest. Dee and Steve Weber (Magic Circle Mining) had their loader buried to the cab with gravel in the creek bed. Dan, Steve's brother, nearly

drowned when he stepped off the bank to retrieve something swirling down the creek and disappeared. Steve reached out his hand to pull Dan back to shore and was hit by a boulder tumbling through the water. Both of them escaped the creek with minor injury. Before the waters began to recede, the creek had eaten the bank away within 6 inches of their camp…

Others on the creeks lost tools, fuel tanks, an outhouse, parts and equipment, but no one was hurt. The road to Circle washed out in 14 places and was under 4 foot of water at Birch Creek. The road between Central and the Springs washed out in two places but was repaired the next morning.

Bruce had to make an emergency run to Frank Warren's mine on Crooked Creek. Mary called him at the Springs in a panic to tell him the brakes on the D-9 were locked up, it was sitting in the creek, and the dike was about to be washed away. Bruce jumped in the service truck and went tearing over to Frank's. He didn't return until after midnight but when he did the Cat was running and out of harm's way. Since the road was washed out he left his service truck in Central and Frank flew him to the Springs. They buzzed the trailer and I groggily went over to meet them. I'd gone to bed just awhile before. In the morning the waters began to drop and weary miners who had kept an all-night vigil guarding their camps began to relax. By noon Deadwood Creek had dropped 6 feet. (Tyler n.d., 1984 entry)

Yet again in 1989, less than twenty years after the last flood, there occurred another hundred-year flood. Lin Gale (1989), a staff writer for the *Fairbanks Daily News-Miner*, discussed the trepidation the rain caused both Chena River residents and the folks from Central on Crooked Creek. She described Crooked Creek as a hundred-foot-wide river, a foot and a half deep, running down the main street. Julie Cooper was an eyewitness to this event. She and her husband, Denny, were living within a quarter-mile of the junction of the Circle Hot Springs Road and the Steese Highway that summer. Julie commented:

Big flood that flooded the road, DOT, and tore up all the pavement there. Ed Gelvin called it the hundred-year flood. Flooded Crabb's

Corner. Jim and Lori Wilde's basement was five feet deep. Frank Warren put big dikes by his house. Central Motor Inn put up a sign that he had River Front Property for sale. Floodwater came in behind us and floated away the dog bowls and moved the dogs into high ground. (Gale 1989)

Julie helped Lori Wilde clean up the mess and the toys from the museum that were covered in mud. The 1989 flood also destroyed the remainder of the old Nation City town site on the left bank of the Yukon River, a few miles downriver of its confluence with the Nation River. Central resident Collette Glanz (2010) offered a personal account of this flood:

In 1989 Bill's daughter was visiting in Central and she went visiting one of the local girls for three days. They got stuck because of the flood. Water washed the Hot Springs too and the whole hillside. BLM station was open and the BLM people were floating around Central in their canoes. The year the Hot Springs flooded, some tourists got stranded there, unable to leave to get back to work. Road was washed out.

Summary

The ethnohistory of Central and its surrounding areas is a story of settlers, mining, trapping, interdependency, and self-sufficiency, as shown through the lives of the Larsen/Olson family members, the Tyrrell family, and the many other miners, freighters, educators, and trappers, including the McQuesten, Rasmussen, Warren, Cherosky, O'Leary, and Oakes families. Due to the conditions encountered by settlers who came from faraway places—in the case of the Larsens, from distant Norway—and the implements for mining supplied by a distant market and inconsistent transportation infrastructure, populations and supplies were in constant flux. Traders were not always able to supply the miners with provisions that would last through the winter (Webb 1985, 84). For this reason, learning how to fish and hunt proved to be essential for survival. Some of the early miners also had to contend with scurvy and occasionally even starvation, especially if they were not independent and skilled enough to live partially off the land (Davis 1967, 44).

The early miners traded with Native people for meat and furs, and the Natives sometimes assisted the miners in hunting (Davis 1967, 45). Many settlers, such as James Carroll, who settled in Fort Yukon, married Native women who were skilled in living in Interior Alaska, and without whose help many would surely have departed the region or perished. Miners also tell about helping Alaska Natives with gifts of food and clothing when hard times, such as the influenza and other epidemics, hit Native community members. For example, in the winter of 1897–1898—called the "starvation winter"—McQuesten had pulled his trading post out and had no food in reserve to trade. A whole group of Natives had come to the region from Tanana to trade but found no food available, so the miners and others in the area scraped together food to help them out.

Within Central in particular, the descendants of the settlers maintain a proudly distinct lifeway that focuses on self-reliance alongside cooperation and mutual concern for well-being. Newcomers must adapt to the unique traditions among more familiar American cultural traditions to make their lives successful, obtaining the necessary provisions for life by way of individual action and interdependent obligations. Central is a community that embodies the values of self-reliance and interdependence, and its important connections with the community of Circle originate from the time of the establishment of both settlements. The self-reliance of the people of Central fosters an independent spirit that we see in their activities and resistance to regulations that are perceived to restrict them. Local self-reliance leads to an attitude of personal freedom—a sort of rugged individualism that stokes the fires of controversy with government officials who operate in a system where the individual is subservient to the policy of the leader. This rugged individualism, however, does not seem to lessen the interdependency in place at the local level.

Central and its community represent a different worldview from that of the indigenous peoples of the central-eastern Interior of Alaska. As shown in this chapter, the values of production and consumption, wealth and resources varied greatly, especially in the early years of contact. Nevertheless, settlers often had to depend on the local, traditional, indigenous knowledge of the Gwichyaa Gwich'in and the Hän Hwëch'in peoples for subsistence, and they in turn came to increasingly depend on the outside goods provided through trade and, later, wage labor. The result of these significant if relatively infrequent cross-cultural encounters and resulting acculturation was a gradual overlapping of some aspects of the worldviews of these peoples, though each retains a distinct culture to the present. The Native heritage of Central is primarily historical, and not necessarily overt, but it is nevertheless present such as in Mary Warren's family and Albert Carroll's ties with his trapping partners and Laurel Tyrrell.

The linkages between Central and Circle are strengthened by way of the important Steese Highway, which connects both communities to Fairbanks (approximately 160 miles to the southwest). Because of the long-established connections created and maintained by proximity, hunting, trapping, and mining, the local histories of Central and Circle are at times inseparable. Now more than ever, interdependency is the condition of life in the rural Interior. In the current era of relative open-mindedness and acceptance of diversity, indigenous cultures are experiencing a cultural revitalization. For the same reasons, this revitalization is culturally affecting the worldviews and lifeways of settlers and their descendants as well, as reflected in values and ethics regarding hunting, fishing, trapping, reciprocity, and community.

FIVE

New Traditions

Subsistence, Commerce, and Shared History

OUR WORK ON this ethnohistorical study has brought the many strands of people within the central-eastern Interior of Alaska and their lifeways into a single volume that demonstrates the connections between them, in spite of, and yet because of, their diversity and heritage. As traditions changed, were abandoned, or created, the peoples of the region relied on one another to survive and thrive. This interdependence is shown to include the sharing of knowledge and expertise as populations met, traded, mixed, and persisted through social and natural upheavals. The people who have, over countless generations (certainly in excess of seven hundred generations), inhabited the lands of the central-eastern Interior have developed traditions that tie them to the land, and to one another. These include the ancestors of today's Hän, Gwichyaa, and Denduu Athabascans, and more recently the many nonindigenous settlers of the region. In more recent times, these diverse peoples have experienced an integration of their cultures, though cultural differences—and the identities associated with these differences—remain. Nevertheless, all peoples have contributed to the syncretic, blended cultural conditions of the present, in part based on demonstrating their worth in self-sufficiency and through sharing.

Long before the arrival of settlers from other lands and other countries, indigenous people interacted with one another as they moved across the land in their seasonal round for subsistence, frequently exchanging ideas, resources, and members. In fact, it has been demonstrated in the past and present that the cultural ethic of sharing has been critical to the successful survival of people and their cultures in this rugged, often-harsh land. Nevertheless, due to a deep and intimate understanding of the nature of the lands, waters, and air, survival was possible within an interdependent relationship. While this relationship existed between individuals and groups, indigenous people also developed relationships with the nonhuman aspects of the environment—in other words, with the nonhuman "people" of this environment, including animals, plants, and inanimate aspects of existence. Not only did this complex and deep spiritual relationship include an inseparability of humans from nature, but its foundation lay in respect—respect for the infinite expressions of existence. In this way, both materially and spiritually, a balanced and sustainable ethic developed and persisted for thousands of years. Such notions of respect are also held by the settler population, but due to differing worldviews, notions of "luck" and "spiritual connectedness" are not as prominent, or manifest differently, though all recognize and praise individual skill and talent.

Though the local condition of interdependence, sharing, and respect has its origins with the region's indigenous people, these ethics have been adopted (and often also already existed) among the settlers who came to call the Yukon–Charley region their home. The often-harsh environmental and climatological conditions necessitate a respect and care that if not followed can lead to difficulties, and even death, whether indigenous or settler. Many of the skills practiced and attitudes held by the people of the region reflect this respect and care, and these admirable traits are often some of the first differences noticed by visitors. Another difference noted by outsiders is the love of freedom and liberty that is expressed by all the people of the region. For many, this is what draws and keeps them here, as has been repeatedly demonstrated by the stories shared in this text.

Within this rich context, the local National Park Service employees of the Yukon–Charley Rivers National Preserve work to maintain the natural and cultural diversity of the region. As identified in its 2010 annual report, the purpose of the preserve is, among others, to "protect, conserve, and interpret natural and cultural resources…while allowing for appropriate human uses in a manner that provides for similar opportunities for future use and enjoyment." Though whether or not this maxim is being upheld is hotly debated in the region, this statement demonstrates that the goals of the preserve include the maintenance of cultural and natural diversity—and uniqueness—in a sustainable way that also preserves the benefits and opportunities for future generations. Further, the preserve's commitment to "protect and interpret historical sites and events associated with the Yukon River gold rush, and geological and paleontological history, and cultural prehistory of [the] area" recognizes that "portions of the Han (Hän) and Kutchin (Gwich'in) Athabaskan traditional homelands lie within the Preserve" and that "sites preserving activities and events of regional significance associated with the gold rush era are present and exemplified by bucket dredges, mail trails, trapper's cabins, boats, roadhouses, water ditches, and machinery," thus recognizing the cultural diversity and historical significance of the region.

Another highly important aspect of the Yukon–Charley Rivers National Preserve and surrounding regions is the reliance on subsistence activities. As was stated by the preserve's subsistence liaison and interpretive ranger, Pat Sanders, "If you don't have it and you need it, you make it, catch it, or do without" (NPS 2010). Some of the resident people of the region, as described in this ethnohistory, continue to actively participate in subsistence activities, reflecting the self-reliance and interdependence that simultaneously reflect and even represent those who dwell here. Due to prohibitive costs of freighting in goods, subsistence is often a necessary, and sometimes critical, activity. But often more than this practical concern, subsistence is an important lifeway for all the people of the region and serves to form identity and meaning in individuals' daily lives.

The National Park Service administrators of the Yukon–Charley Rivers National Preserve almost exclusively live and work in Fairbanks, though in addition to Pat Sanders there are a few other local employees hired seasonally or temporarily. Due to rigorous law enforcement policies, or regulations that provide no latitude for changing circumstances (which is a hallmark of subsistence activities), unfulfilled promises, and a feeling that "outsiders" are telling "insiders" how to live their lives, there is considerable local distrust of the National Park Service employees in general and of the nonlocal employees in particular. It must be noted, though, that this is not a universal perspective and that many people are essentially indifferent. Few openly support the park service and its agendas, however, and there is a feeling of unacceptable intrusiveness. Resistance to NPS policies and initiatives has increasingly become a feature of local identity—a way to passively oppose the power of an impersonal, nonlocal government bureaucracy that nevertheless possesses and exercises regulatory powers over the region.

In spite of the challenge inherent in the changes that accompany the establishment of a federally managed preserve, local residents strive to find common ground with the National Park Service for the greater benefit of the surrounding environs and the communities supported by the preserve and the efforts of its genuinely dedicated local employees. Local resident Don Woodruff notes that the preserve office set up a Subsistence Resource Commission (SRC) so that the park service must interact with the community and therefore build trust. Time is usually provided to discuss issues as they come up, instead of arbitrarily making enforcement decisions. Don emphasizes that people on the land are the best (that is, most knowledgeable) stewards, and therefore they are the best consultants when park service employees need information about the land, the water, and the animals.

As an ethnohistorical document, this work focuses on the lives of the residents of Alaska's central-eastern Interior, and as such, much effort has been directed toward an account of their historical and contemporary practices. This work also explores the personal accounts of the region's inhabitants and their efforts to define themselves and maintain their identities in a time of rapid cultural, social, and environmental change, accomplished by providing a space for local people to tell their own history from their own perspective. The connections between the people and the land—a tie that runs very deep indeed—are demonstrated through the written and oral histories and stories of the people of the region. An effort has been made to blend existing accounts and research—both oral and written—with the personal perspectives of current lifelong or long-term residents. The influence of these local residents is evident, and as a cultural and historical document, this effort strives to respect the interests and perspectives of the people who are its focus.

The lives of the ancestors of today's people shaped the way people live today, and in the central-eastern Interior this historical and cultural heritage is richly remembered. The presence of the Circle District Historical Society and Museum in Central and the Eagle Historical Society and Museums in Eagle attest to this fascination with, and the importance of, the past in defining the identities of the present. These historical institutions work to preserve the knowledge of the past and the present in order to demonstrate the connections that are continuous, including heritage and tradition. By recognizing that the actions of ancestors of past generations shape the nature of life in the present, the people of Alaska's central-eastern Interior are aware that their actions and values in the present will shape the nature of generations still to come.

Fundamental to this ethnohistory is the repeatedly demonstrated importance of sharing and relationships, and how this can be applied in various ways to mutual advantage, including in the creation and telling of a "people's history." Through the focus on the communities of Eagle, Central, and Circle as case studies, we have shown how sharing— particularly in times of crisis—and relationships built over time led to a condition of sustainable interdependency, a condition not readily or easily attained cross-culturally, and rarely seen in colonial-settler contexts. Perhaps due to the earlier colonial experiences of the nonindigenous settlers of Alaska, maybe due to the ethics and values of the region's indigenous peoples, and hopefully due to a common recognition of each other's humanity, the colonial experience in the eastern Interior was relatively amicable, and some local Gwich'in have remarked with pride that they never resisted settlers with violence, and likewise they themselves were never conquered.

We conclude with this observation: in Alaska's central-eastern Interior, indigenous Alaskan and settler people's mutual and cooperative influence, albeit not without stresses and challenges, led to current conditions of interdependence—an outcome that is notably rare in the world, and that is especially rare in the history of the United States in regard to indigenous North Americans. Though the indigenous and settler communities remain more or less physically separated, cooperation continues between communities and between populations within communities. The pressures of harsh climate and rugged landscape pushed indigenous and settler cultures together for purposes of survival, and for their mutual benefit. Cooperation, tolerance, respect, and resulting interdependence resulted in an outcome that is more than the sum of its parts, and that serves to inform other regions of mixed indigenous and colonial populations on strategies for mutual survival. We hope that further research into other successful conditions of multicultural communities and cross-cultural exchange within a society can demonstrate strategies for moving forward from often-inequitable historical conditions toward a mutually beneficial future based on mutual acceptance. We feel the people of the communities in Alaska's central-eastern Interior are accomplishing this laudable achievement.

References Cited

Aho, Karen

    1996   "Twelve Ounces of Gold Stolen from Central Museum." *Fairbanks Daily News-Miner*, August 16.

Adams, Charles W.

    2002   *A Cheechako Goes to the Klondike*. Kenmore, WA: Epicenter Press.

Adney, Tappan

    1898   "A Winter's Work in the Klondike: Letter and Illustrations." *Harper's Weekly*: 960–963.

    1900   "Moose Hunting with the Tro-chu-tin." *Harper's New Monthly Magazine* 100, no. 598: 494–507.

Alder, Lee

    1973   "Central Highlights." *Fairbanks Daily News-Miner*, November 2.

Andersen, David B.

    1974   *Regional Geography of the Central Area. Geography 327 Research Paper. University of Alaska*. Circle District Historical Society Archives 87-A-6-1.

    1992   *The Use of Dog Teams and the Use of Subsistence Caught Fish for Feeding Sled Dogs in the Yukon River Drainage, Alaska*. Juneau: Alaska Department of Fish and Game, Division of Subsistence. Technical paper.

Associated Press

    2009   "Yukon River Recedes in Eagle After Ice Jam Breaks." *Anchorage Daily News,* May 7.

Axtell, James

1979   "Ethnohistory: An Historian's Viewpoint." *Ethnohistory* 26, no. 1 (winter): 1–13.

Beckstead, Douglas

2003   *The World Turned Upside Down: A History of Mining on Coal Creek and Woodchopper Creek, Yukon–Charley Rivers National Preserve.* Fairbanks: US Dept. of the Interior, National Park Service.

Berton, Pierre

2001   *Klondike: The Last Great Gold Rush 1896–1899.* Toronto: Anchor Canada.

Bishop, Sam

1986   "Residents Ask: Why Upgrade Steese, Then Not Keep It Open?" *Fairbanks Daily News-Miner*, January 25.

Blackhouse, Frances

1995   *Women of the Klondike.* Vancouver: Whitecap Books.

Brown, Jennifer S. H.

1980   *Strangers in Blood: Fur Trade Company Families in Indian Country.* Vancouver: University of British Columbia Press.

Bureau of Land Management

1999   *Eagle–Fort Egbert: A Remnant of the Past.* Fairbanks: Bureau of Land Management and the Eagle Historical Society and Museum, BLM Alaska Adventures in the Past Series, no. 5.

Callahan, Erinia Pavaloff Cherosky

1975   "A Yukon Autobiography." *Alaska Journal* 5, no. 2: 127–128.

Carroll, James A.

1957   *The First Ten Years in Alaska: Memoirs of a Fort Yukon trapper, 1911–1922.* New York: Exposition Press.

2005   *Above the Arctic Circle: The Journals of James A. Carroll 1911–1922.* Anchorage: Publications Consultants.

Caulfield, Richard

1979   *Subsistence Use in and around the Proposed Yukon–Charley National Rivers.* Fairbanks: Anthropology and Historic Preservation, Cooperative Park Studies Unit, University of Alaska Fairbanks.

Coates, Ken, and Bill Morrison

1990 *The Sinking of the Princess Sophia: Taking the North Down with Her.* Toronto: Oxford University Press.

Cox, Jody

2000 "The Upper Yukon River, the Salmon and the People: A History of Salmon Fisheries." Unpublished draft. Prepared for Parks Canada, US National Park Service, and Tr'ondek Hwech'in.

Cruikshank, Julie

1979 *Athapaskan Women: Lives and Legends.* Ottawa: National Museums of Canada.

Darbyshire and Associates

1990a Central. Juneau: Department of Community and Regional Affairs, Division of Municipal and Regional Assistance.

1990b Central. Juneau: Department of Community and Regional Affairs, Division of Municipal and Regional Assistance.

Davis, Henry

1967 "Recollections." In *Sourdough Sagas.* Cleveland and New York: The World Publishing Company.

Dee, Jay

1939 "In Memoriam." *The Alaska Miner*, April 4.

Dobrowolsky, Helene

2008 *Hammerstones: A History of the Tr'ondek Hwech'in.* Dawson City, Yukon: Tr'ondek Hwech'in Publication.

Downing, Suzanne

2017 "John Sturgeon, Hunter, Likely Heading Back to Supreme Court." *Must Read Alaska*, http://mustreadalaska.com/john-sturgeon-hunter-likely-heading-back-supreme-court/, October 5, 2017, accessed November 29, 2017.

Ducker, James H.

1982 "Alaska's Upper Yukon Region: A History." Unpublished draft. Anchorage: Bureau of Land Management.

Dunham, Samuel C.

1898 "The Alaskan Goldfields and the Opportunities They Offer for Capital and Labor." In *Bulletin of the Department of Labor*, edited by

Carroll D. Wright. US Congress, House. Document 206, pt. 3. 55th Cong., 2d sess..

Ferguson, Judy

1999 "Carrying Their Load, Early Mail Carriers Found the Will and the Way." In Northland News (February), 9–13. *Fairbanks Daily News-Miner.*

Firth, John

1998 *Yukon Quest: The 1000-Mile Dog Sled Race Through the Yukon and Alaska.* Whitehorse, Yukon: Lost Moose.

Flannigan, M. D., B. J. Stocks, and B. M. Wotton

2000 "Climate Change and Forest Fires." *The Science of the Total Environment* 262: 221–229.

Freeman, Louise

2011 "Rebuilding Eagle Village: Community Rises Anew from Yukon River Ice, Flood Devastation." *Fairbanks Daily News-Miner,* November 27.

Gale, Lin

1989 "Rains Keep Area Residents Wary." *Fairbanks Daily News-Miner,* June 26.

Gates, Michael

1994 *Gold at Fortymile Creek, Early Days in the Yukon.* Vancouver: UBC Press.

Griffin, Kristen P.

1988 *An Overview and Assessment of Prehistoric Archaeological Resources, Yukon–Charley Rivers National Preserve, Alaska.* Anchorage: US Dept. of the Interior, National Park Service, Alaska Regional Office.

Gruening, Ernest

1968 *State of Alaska.* New York: Random House.

Gwich'in Council International

2010. Retrieved October 10, 2012, https://gwichincouncil.com/gwichin.

Haigh, Jane

1996 "And His Native Wife. Preserving and Interpreting Cultural Change." *Proceedings of the Alaska Historical Society Annual Meeting:* 39–54.

Hall, E. S., Jr.

1976 "Aboriginal Occupations of the Charley River and Adjacent Yukon River Drainage, East-Central Alaska." In *The Environment of the Yukon–Charley Rivers Area, Alaska*, edited by Steven Young. Wolcott, VT: Center for Northern Studies.

Harbo, Lisa

1996 "A House Called Miller, a Family Called Kelly." Heartland insert, H9–H13. *Fairbanks Daily News-Miner*, April 21.

Hartman, Brian, and Gerd Wendler

2005 "The Significance of the 1976 Pacific Climate Shift in the Climatology of Alaska." *Journal of Climate* 18, no. 24: 4824–4839.

Haskell, William B.

1997 *Two Years in the Klondike and Alaskan Gold Fields 1896–1898*. Fairbanks: University of Alaska Press.

Hay, Majorie J.

1976 "Circle City Pioneer Rasmussen House Stands as Memory." *Fairbanks Daily News-Miner*, March 20.

Haynes, Terry L., and William E. Simeone

2007 *Upper Tanana Ethnographic Overview and Assessment, Wrangell–St. Elias National Park and Preserve*. Juneau: Alaska Department of Fish and Game, Division of Subsistence. Technical paper.

Hinzman, Larry D., et al.

2005 "Evidence and Implications of Recent Climate Change in Northern Alaska and Other Arctic Regions." *Climatic Change* 72: 251–298.

Hughes, Vic

1991 "Yukon Quest, Blend of Yesterday and Today." *Yukon Quest Annual*.

Isto, Sarah Crawford

2007 *Good Company: A Mining Family in Fairbanks, Alaska*. Fairbanks: University of Alaska Press.

Jeglum, Connie

2005 *A Brief History of the People Buried in the Central Cemetery Near Central, Alaska*. Fairbanks: The Fairbanks Genealogical Society.

Johnson, Linda

2009 *The Kandik Map*. Fairbanks: University of Alaska Press.

Jorgenson, M. Torre, et al.

2001 "Permafrost Degradation and Ecological Changes Associated with a Warming Climate in Central Alaska." *Climatic Change* 48: 551–579.

Juneby-Potts, Adeline

1993 *Walk by the Spirit, Including Our Last and Best Season on the Trapline by Mike Potts.* Laramie, WY: Jelm Mountain Press.

Kaye, Roger

1992 "Northland News" (May), 9. *Fairbanks Daily News-Miner.*

Koskey, Michael

2007 *Subsistence Resource Use Among Ten Tanana River Valley Communities: 2004–2005.* Juneau: Alaska Department of Fish and Game, Division of Subsistence. Technical paper.

2009 *Traditional Ecological Knowledge and Biological Sampling of Non-Salmon Fish Species in the Yukon Flats Region, Alaska.* Juneau: Alaska Department of Fish and Game, Division of Subsistence. Technical paper.

Kosuta, Kathy

1988 *Han Indians: People of the River.* Dawson City, Yukon: Dawson Indian Band.

Lattery, Dennis

2008 *Hunts and Home Fires: Surviving 50 Years of Alaska and Other Interesting Things.* Anchorage: Publication Consultants.

L'Ecuyer, Rosalie, and Lael Morgan

1996 "The Inner Circle, Faces of Early Mining District Fill in Historical Gap." Heartland Insert H8–H13. *Fairbanks Daily News-Miner,* December 1.

Leo, Richard

1996 *Way Out Here.* Seattle: Sasquatch Books.

Lurie, Nancy O.

1961 "Ethnohistory: An Ethnological Point of View." *Ethnohistory* 8, no. 1 (winter): 78–92.

Lyle, W. M.

1973 "Geologic and Mineral Evaluation of the Charley River Drainage, Alaska." State of Alaska Department of Natural Resources,

Division of Geological and Geophysical Surveys, Alaska Open File Report 28.

Lynge, Finn
1992 *Arctic Wars, Animal Rights and Endangered Peoples*. Hanover, NH: University Press of New England.

Marcus, Joel, Eric Veach, Molly McCormick, and Ray Hander
2004 *Freshwater Fish Inventory of Denali National Park and Preserve, Wrangell–St. Elias National Park and Preserve, and Yukon–Charley Rivers National Preserve, Central Alaska Inventory and Monitoring Network*. Wrangell–St. Elias National Park and Preserve. Copper Center, AK.

McKennan, Robert Addison
1966 "Athapaskan Groups of Central Alaska at the Time of White Contact." Moscow: Presentation at the VIIth International Congress of Anthropological and Ethnological Sciences.

McMahan, David J., and Charles E. Holmes
1985 *Cultural Resources Survey: Taylor Highway Mile 110 to Mile 153*. Alaska Division of Geological and Geophysical Surveys Public Data File 85-58.

McPhee, John
1976 *Coming into the Country*. New York: Farrar, Straus, and Giroux.

Miller, Hunter (ed.)
1931 *Treaties and Other International Acts of the United States of America*. Vol. 2, Documents 1–40: 1776–1818. Washington, DC: Government Printing Office.

Mishler, Craig W., and Charles E. Holmes
1983 *Cultural Resources Survey: Eagle Village to Dog Island*. Juneau: Alaska Dept. of Natural Resources, Alaska Division of Geological and Geophysical Surveys.

Mercier, François Xavier
1986 *Recollection of the Youkon: Memoires from the Years 1868–1885*. Anchorage: Alaska Historical Society.

Mishler, Craig, and William Simeone
2004 *Han, People of the River: Han Hwech'in, an Ethnography and Ethnohistory*. Fairbanks: University of Alaska Press.

Mowry, Tim

2010a "Do You Have What It Takes for Hot Springs 100?" *Fairbanks Daily News-Miner*, June 9.

2010b "National Park Service Rangers Arrest 70-Year-Old Central Man." *Fairbanks Daily News-Miner*, September 27.

2010c "Future of Fortymile Caribou Hunt to Be Determined Next Week." *Fairbanks Daily News-Miner*, November 11.

Murray, Alexander Hunter

1910 *Journal of the Yukon, 1847–48*. Ottawa: Government Printing Bureau.

National Park Service, US Department of the Interior

2005 *Yukon–Charley Rivers National Preserve Annual Report, 2005*. Yukon–Charley Rivers National Preserve. Fairbanks, Alaska.

2006 *Yukon–Charley Rivers National Preserve Annual Report, 2006*. Yukon–Charley Rivers National Preserve. Fairbanks, Alaska.

2007 *Yukon–Charley Rivers National Preserve Annual Report, 2007*. Yukon–Charley Rivers National Preserve. Fairbanks, Alaska.

2008 *Yukon–Charley Rivers National Preserve Annual Report, 2008*. Yukon–Charley Rivers National Preserve. Fairbanks, Alaska.

2010 *Yukon–Charley Rivers National Preserve Annual Report, 2010*. Yukon–Charley Rivers National Preserve. Fairbanks, Alaska.

Nelson, Richard K.

1986 *Hunters of the Northern Forest*. 2nd ed. Chicago: University of Chicago Press.

Nickels, Bryan

2001 "Native American Free Passage Rights Under the 1794 Jay Treaty: Survival Under United States Statutory Law and Canadian Common Law." *Boston College International and Comparative Law Review* 24, no. 2: article 5.

Oakes, Patricia

1983 *Birch Creek and the Circle Mining District, Alaska: Historical Overview of an Economic Entity*. Central, AK: New Yukon Press.

1984 "History—The Circle District." In *Yukon Quest Annual: 1984 Fairbanks to Whitehorse*, edited by Gretchen Walker

1986　*Supporting Year-round Maintenance of the Steese Highway.* Central, AK: Oakeservices.

O'Harra, Doug

1993　"The Feud on Crazy Mountain, When the Homestead Dream Turned Bad." *We Alaskans,* the *Anchorage Daily News* magazine.

O'Neill, Dan

2006　*A Land Gone Lonesome.* New York: Counterpoint.

Orth, Donald J.

1967　*Dictionary of Alaska Place Names.* USGS Professional Paper 567. US Department of the Interior. Washington, DC: US Government Printing Office.

Osgood, Cornelius

1971　*The Han Indians: A Compilation of Ethnographic and Historical Data on the Alaska-Yukon Boundary Area.* New Haven, CT: Department of Anthropology, Yale University.

Pahlke, Loren G.

1985　*On Two Frontiers: White Social Structure in the Alaskan Bush.* Boulder: University of Colorado.

Porter, Elmer Alfred, and Clarence Eugene Ellsworth

1912　*Mining and Water-Supply of Fortymile, Seventymile, Circle, and Fairbanks Districts, Alaska in 1911.* Geological Survey Bulletin. Washington, DC US Government Printing Office.

Prindle, L. M.

1905　"The Fortymile Gold Placer District." *Bulletin* 345: 179–186.

Raboff, Adeline, and James Kari

2011　*Compilation of Yukon Flats Athabascan Place Names for Stevens Village, Beaver, Birch Creek and Fort Yukon.* Fairbanks: Alaska Native Language Center.

Ramseur, David

1980　"Local Riders Hit a Gold Dust Trail." *Fairbanks Daily News-Miner,* July 19.

Reynolds, Louise, and James Jordan

1983　*Archeological Reconnaissance of the Yukon–Charley Rivers National Preserve.* Anchorage: National Park Service, Alaska Region.

Rooth, Anna Birgitta

1971 *The Alaska Expedition 1966: Myths, Customs, and Beliefs among the Athabascan Indians and the Eskimos of Northern Alaska*. Lund, Sweden: CWK Gleeup, Acta Universitatis Lundensis, Section I:14.

Sapir, Edward

1915 "The Na-Dene Languages: A Preliminary Report." *American Anthropology* 17: 534–558.

Schmit, Robert E.

2015 *Chief Isaac Juneby and the Hell Dogs School: International and Cross-Cultural Conversations. Observations on Education: Mushing Sled Dogs into Cyberspace*. Xulon Press.

Schmitter, Ferdinand

1985 *Upper Yukon Native Customs and Folklore*. Anchorage: Alaska Historical Commission.

Schneider, William

1986 *The Life I've Been Living: By Moses Cruikshank*. Fairbanks: University of Alaska Press.

2012 *On Time Delivery: The Dog Team Mail Carriers*. Fairbanks: University of Alaska Press.

Schwatka, Frederick

1983 "Along Alaska's Great River." Insert in *The Alaska Journal* 13, no. 3. Anchorage: Alaska Northwest Publishing Company.

1885 *Report of a Military Reconnaissance in Alaska in 1883*. Washington, DC: Government Printing Office.

Scott, Elva R.

1997 *Jewel on the Yukon: Eagle City. Collection of Essays on Historic Eagle and Its People*. Eagle, AK: Eagle Historical Society and Museums.

Serreze, M. C., et al.

2000 "Observational Evidence of Recent Change in the Northern High Latitude Environment." *Climate Change* 46: 159–207.

Shinkwin, Anne D., and Russell H. Sackett

1976 *Report on Excavations at US Courthouse, Eagle, Alaska, 1976*. Fairbanks: University of Alaska Fairbanks. Bureau of Land Management, Fortymile Resource Area.

Shinkwin, Anne D., Russell H. Sackett, and Mary V. Kroul

    1978 "Fort Egbert and the Eagle Historic District: Results of Archeological and Historic Research, summer 1977." Prepared for the US Department of the Interior, Bureau of Land Management, Fortymile Resource Area—Tok, Alaska. University of Alaska Anthropology Program, Fairbanks.

Simeone, William

    2007 "The Arrival: Native and Missionary Relations on the Upper Tanana River, 1914." *Alaska Journal of Anthropology* 5, no. 1: 83–94.

Simmons, William C.

    1988 "Culture Theory in Contemporary Ethnohistory." *Ethnohistory* 35, no. 1 (winter): 1–14.

Slobodin, Richard

    1963 "Notes on Han. Appendix II to Preliminary Report on Ethnographic Work, 1962." Unpublished manuscript. Ottawa: National Museum of Man, Ethnology Division.

    1981 "Kutchin." In *Handbook of North American Indians: Subarctic* (vol. 6), edited by W. C. Sturtevant, 514–532. Washington, DC: Smithsonian Institution.

Spurr, J. E., H. B. Goodrich, and F. C. Schrader

    1898 *18th Annual Report of the US Geological Survey.* Washington, DC: US Geological Survey, Department of the Interior.

State of Alaska

    1984 *Steese Highway Central to Circle City Environmental Assessment.* State of Alaska Department of Transportation and Public Facilities Northern Region. Fairbanks: State of Alaska.

Swanson, David K.

    2001 *Ecological Units of Yukon–Charley Rivers National Preserve, Alaska.* Yukon–Charley Rivers National Preserve. Fairbanks.

Tremblay, Ray

    1983 *Trails of an Alaska Trapper.* Anchorage: Alaska Northwest Publishing Company.

Tyrrell, Laurel

    1995 *Stories of a Place.* Unpublished collections.

2002 "Living the Frontier Myth in the Twenty-First Century." Unpublished master's thesis. University of Alaska Fairbanks.

Walden, Arthur T.

1928 *A Dog Puncher on the Yukon*. Cambridge, MA: The Riverside Press.

Webb, Melody

1977 *Yukon Frontiers: Historic Resource Study of the Proposed Yukon–Charley National River*. Fairbanks: Anthropology and Historic Preservation, Cooperative Park Studies Unit, University of Alaska.

1980 *Eagle: Focus on the Yukon*. US National Park Service, Department of the Interior.

1985 *The Last Frontier*. Albuquerque: University of New Mexico Press.

Wickersham, James

1938 *Old Yukon: Tales, Trails, and Trials*. Washington, DC: Washington Law Book Co.

Wilcox, Ted

1985 "Volunteers Have Big Plans, Central Museum Fits Right In." *Fairbanks Daily News-Miner*, July 5.

Wold, Jo Anne

1989 "The Sinking of the Princess Sophia." *Fairbanks Daily News-Miner*, April 23.

Woodman, Lyman (ed.)

1982 *The Opening of Alaska, 1901–1903. By Brigadier General William L. Mitchell, US Army Air Corps*. Anchorage: Cook Inlet Historical Society.

Interviews

Ames, Albert

2011 Interview. Anchorage: Yukon–Charley Rivers National Preserve Ethnographic Overview and Assessment Project. 12/29/10.

Ames, Molly

2011 Interview. Nenana: Yukon–Charley Rivers National Preserve Ethnographic Overview and Assessment Project. 12/31/10.

Bell, Ray
   1991   Interview. Fairbanks: UAF Oral History Program. H91-22-41.
Bertoson, Gordon
   1991   Interview. Fairbanks: UAF Oral History Program. H91-22-53, 54.
Biederman, Charlie
   1995   Interview. Fairbanks: UAF Oral History Program. H95-14.
Biederman, Horace, Jr.
   1976   Interview, 18 September. Yukon Frontiers Historic Resource Study of the Proposed Yukon–Charley Rivers National Preserve. Eagle: National Park Service.
Boquist, Helge
   1995   Interview. Fairbanks: UAF Oral History Program. H95-17.
Borg, John
   2009   Interview. Anchorage: Yukon–Charley Rivers National Preserve Ethnographic Overview and Assessment Project. 11/4/09.
Brown, Randy
   1991   Interview. Fairbanks: UAF Oral History Program. H91-22-42 and H91-22-57, 58.
Carroll, Albert
   2010.   Interview. Circle, Alaska.
Cook, Alfred
   2010   Interview. Central: Yukon–Charley Rivers National Preserve Ethnographic Overview and Assessment Project. 5/7/10.
Evans, Dave
   1991   Interview. Fairbanks: UAF Oral History Program. H91-22-40, 41.
Glanz, William, and Colette Glanz
   2010   Interview. Central: Yukon–Charley Rivers National Preserve Ethnographic Overview and Assessment Project. 8/20/10.
Hansen, Barney, Ole Hansen, and Horace Biederman
   1965   Interview. Fairbanks: UAF Oral History Program. H97-66-11.
Heath, Pat
   1994   Oral history interview. Fairbanks: National Park Service.

Howe and Brown
    1991   Interview. Fairbanks: UAF Oral History Program. H91-22-01.
John, Charles
    2011   Interview. Fairbanks: Yukon–Charley Rivers National Preserve Ethnographic Overview and Assessment Project. 10/31/10.
Juneby, Isaac
    2010   Interview, October 26. Eagle, Alaska.
Kelly, Carolyn
    1991   Interview. Fairbanks: UAF Oral History Program. H91-22-47.
Malcolm, Matthew
    1991   Interview. Fairbanks: UAF Oral History Program. H91-22-18.
Malcolm, Matthew, and Martha Malcolm
    1995   Interview. Fairbanks: UAF Oral History Program. H95-69-06.
McDougal, Michael
    2009   Interview. Eagle: Yukon–Charley Rivers National Preserve Ethnographic Overview and Assessment Project. 11/25/09.
McMullen, Terry
    2011   Interview. Eagle: Yukon–Charley Rivers National Preserve Ethnographic Overview and Assessment Project. 2/27/11.
Miller, Robert
    2010   Interview. Central: Yukon–Charley Rivers National Preserve Ethnographic Overview and Assessment Project. 7/15/10.
O'Leary, George, and Frank Warren
    2008   Interview. Fairbanks: UAF Oral History Program.
Olson, Ruth Larsen
    1996   Interview. Fairbanks: UAF Oral History Program. H96-03-01, H96-03-02.
Ordway, Theresa
    2010   Interview. Central: Yukon–Charley Rivers National Preserve Ethnographic Overview and Assessment Project. 5/20/10.
Patton, Sage
    1991   Interview. Fairbanks: UAF Oral History Program. H91–22–38.
Paul, Louise, and Ruth Ridley
    1991   Interview. Fairbanks: UAF Oral History Program. H91-22-43 and H91-22-63.

Ricks, Melvin B.

1965 *Directory of Alaska Post Offices and Postmasters 1867–1963*. Ketchikan, AK: Tongass Publishing Co.

Ridley, Ruth

2011 Interview. Fairbanks: Yukon–Charley Rivers National Preserve Ethnographic Overview and Assessment Project. 12/31/10.

Roberts, Lynette

1991 Interview. Fairbanks: UAF Oral History Program. H91-22-51, 52, and H95-13.

Sager, Sonja

2009 Interview. Eagle: Yukon–Charley Rivers National Preserve Ethnographic Overview and Assessment Project. 11/25/09.

Sanders, Mary Patricia

2009 Interview. Eagle: Yukon–Charley Rivers National Preserve Ethnographic Overview and Assessment Project.

2011 Interpretive Ranger, Yukon–Charley Rivers National Preserve, National Park Service, Eagle, Alaska. Personal communication. 11/6/09.

Smith, Richard, and Paul Nathaniel

1991 Interview. Fairbanks: UAF Oral History Program. H91-22-09.

Stockbridge, Joyce

1998 Interview. Fairbanks: UAF Oral History Program. H98-18-04.

Stout, Al

1991 Interview. Fairbanks: UAF Oral History Program. H91-22-13.

Straub, Fronzie

1995 Interview. Fairbanks: UAF Oral History Program. H95-30.

Tyrrell, Richard

2010 Interview. Central: Yukon–Charley Rivers National Preserve Ethnographic Overview and Assessment Project. 5/21/10.

Ulvi, Steve

1991 Interview. Fairbanks: UAF Oral History Program. H95-8.

1995 Interview. Fairbanks: UAF Oral History Program. H91-22-05, 06, 07.

Warren, Mary

1995 Interview. Fairbanks: UAF Oral History Program. H95-09-01, H95-09-02.

Wilde, Hannelore
    2010   Interview. Central: Yukon–Charley Rivers National Preserve Ethnographic Overview and Assessment Project. 6/1/10.

Williams, Jane
    2010   Interview. Fairbanks: Yukon–Charley Rivers National Preserve Ethnographic Overview and Assessment Project.

Williams, Paul
    2013   Gwich'in Traditional Chief, Beaver, Alaska. Personal communication. Beaver, Alaska.

Woodruff, Donald
    2011   Interview. Eagle: Yukon–Charley Rivers National Preserve Ethnographic Overview and Assessment Project. 2/27/11.

Archival

Alaska Community Database Online (ACDO). Alaska Division of Community and Regional Affairs. Alaska Department of Commerce, Community, and Economic Development, State of Alaska, Juneau.

Babcock, Patricia Rae
    n.d.   "History of the Horse in the Circle District from 1898–1930s."

Behr, April
    n.d.   "Mr. Williams Tells It the Way It Was." *The Wolverine Whisper*, Far North School, Central, Alaska. Volume 3(1): 6.

Bowen, Richard J.
    1956   Personal Papers of Bowen, R. J. (Richard John), 1890–1907, R. J. Bowen fonds, General Synod Archives, Toronto: Anglican Church of Canada.

Cacy, Robert J.
    2004   "Frank Leach: Alaska Stories." Unpublished digital recordings.

Circle District Historical Society, Inc., Newsletter
    n.d.   Vol. I, no. 1.
    n.d.   "Some Dates to Remember." New Yukon Press and Oakeservices.
    1993   "Monte Carlo Raises $2400 for Society." Vol. xi, no. 1: 2.
    1993   "Staking and Naming Claims in the Birch Creek Mining District." Vol. xi, no. 1: 4–5.

Edgerton, H. H., Jr.

    1907   Maps 1907 Road Built Circle City to Miller House. Central, AK: Circle District Historical Society Museum.

Flewelling, Fredrick Fairweather

    1898   Journal, 1896–1897.

Hog, Norma J.

    1931   Personal Letter to Mother.

Hunston, Jeffrey

    1978   "Archaeological Survey in the Pelly River Drainage, and Excavations at Moosehide Site (LaVk-2), Central Yukon Territory, 1977." Unpublished manuscript on file, University of Alaska, Archaeology Laboratory, Anchorage.

Olson, Ruth Larsen

    n.d.   Photo collections. Circle District Historical Society.

    n.d.   Unpublished memoirs provided by the family and Circle District Historical Society.

Pioneers of Alaska Grand Igloo #4

    2009   "Riverboats and Golden Dreams Celebrating 100 Years of Igloo #4." Fairbanks: September 16–19, 2009, Convention.

Tyler, Constance

    n.d.   Personal Diary of Constance Tyler: History of the 1984 Flood.

About the Authors

MICHAEL KOSKEY is an assistant professor with the University of Alaska Fairbanks's Center for Cross-Cultural Studies, which offers a master of arts in cross-cultural studies and a PhD in indigenous studies. Mike was born in Germany and moved to Florida as a child. He was an exchange student to Wales, United Kingdom, in high school and joined the US Marine Corps upon graduation. He received a BS in anthropology and a BA in political science from the University of Central Florida, an MS in anthropology from Purdue University, and a PhD in anthropology from University of Alaska Fairbanks.

Mike's research focuses on oral history, traditional knowledge, ethnohistory, culture change, decolonization, resource use and allocation, and indigenous cosmology and mythology. Research areas include the cultures of indigenous peoples in Alaska and neighboring Yukon Territory, Canada—particularly among the Hän and Gwich'in peoples. Mike has done ethnographic and/or archaeological fieldwork in Belize, Florida, Indiana, eastern Siberia, and throughout Alaska. Mike participates in hunting and fishing annually, including extended stays each summer at a Yukon River fish camp with friends from the region.

LAUREL TYRRELL has been an active participant in a subsistence lifestyle for approximately forty years. She follows a seasonal calendar, moving from place to place harvesting game animals and edible plants. Each move is dependent upon natural factors such as breakup and freeze-up as well as regulatory factors such as the opening and closing of moose or caribou season. During the winter, she primarily lives and works on a trapline apart from any community located within the Yukon Flats National Wildlife Refuge. Laurel spends the months of June and July predominantly at the two-story log cabin she built with her husband six miles from the community of Central. Early to mid-August begins the large-game harvest season, first caribou and then moose. Laurel harvests animals primarily from the Porcupine caribou herd, and she and her family move to the Arctic National Wildlife Refuge during this time and live in a tent camp until the season ends or they harvest enough meat to last until the next harvest season. By the end of September she moves back to the Central cabin to gather and process meat and other food, supplies, and equipment repair needed for the next six months on the trapline.

Laurel earned a BS in education from Wheelock College in Boston, Massachusetts. In 2002, she obtained her master's degree in northern studies from the University of Alaska Fairbanks.

VARPU LOTVONEN is a doctoral student in the Department of Anthropology at the University of Alaska Fairbanks. She is from Finland and first came to Alaska as an exchange student during her studies for her master's degree, during which she worked among the Sámi people, followed by her work as a research assistant in Alaska on the project from which this text is derived. In her current PhD work, Varpu is focusing on the experiences and the ethnohistory of the migration of some Sámi families and their reindeer from northern Fennoscandia to Alaska in the early twentieth century.

Index